I'm on a Journey to See You, Sam

Jack Waddington

ISBN: 978-1-9194404-4-6   Printed in the European Union.

ShadowScript Publications uses paper sourced only from sustainable forestry. Viva la forests!

ShadowScript Publications is committed to diversity, inclusion and equality.

Front and back cover illustrations by Jack Waddington. Text layout by Niall MacGiolla Bhuí.

www.shadowscriptwordsmiths.com

Table of Contents

SHOCK

SUNDAY 3 MARCH

I'm on a journey to see you, Sam. You're not alive, but I'm coming to see you. I'm your brother – forever and ever – and I need to see you one last time. I'm on the train now, pulling out of London – Waterloo to Beastly Eastleigh. Back to my home away from home. It's all dark and unfamiliar outside. I'm about to experience something new, something abnormal, and it fills me with dread. No turning back now, though. This is it. My jaw's tense, my knees are numb. I'm not ready for a new chapter. A new life. A life without you.

Shit.

***

You're my god, Sam. The thing high up in the sky. That's you. Soaring above the clouds in your electric wheelchair, your magic carpet. You made my world, and I love you for that. You had faith in people, faith in life. Unlike me. I have little faith in many things. But I'll keep talking to you. I won't be closing my eyes, bowing my head, and thanking you for the food on my plate. I won't be confessing my sins either. We'll just talk, like we're doing now. Speaking with you over the phone was my therapy. Every day, after teaching at school. Hearing your low, gravelly voice talk me through what you'd been doing that day. Crossing my fingers you weren't in too much pain – Duchenne was a bitch to live with. Especially as you got older.

I won't stop this treatment.

Let's keep on chatting nonsense. We'll laugh and be serious and consider lots of different things. From your disability and the difficulties that came with it, to my mental health and fuzzy future. Anything we want to talk about; we'll talk the crap out of it. You'll always be here for me, Sam, even if you're not *here* here.

***

You died at home just over two hours ago. No one saw it coming.

I was enjoying a bowl of spaghetti Agathe had cooked when Dad called around seven-thirty. He told me you were in a coma. I couldn't believe it. Comas are things that happen on TV, not in real life. You were meant to be eternal, not terminal, regardless of what silly muscle-wasting condition you had.

Not knowing if you'd be alive by the time I made it to Hampshire – but knowing I had to see you – I quickly packed a suitcase, said goodbye to Agathe, and left the flat. As I hurried through the dark streets towards West Acton tube station, I got another call from Dad. He told me you'd stopped breathing. I stopped dragging my suitcase.

'What do you—I don't get it.'

'He's gone, Jack.'

Something left my body. You, I think, Sam. It was as if a vacuum had sucked you out of my chest. I felt lighter, half-empty. My hands and legs shook so violently I could barely hold my phone. For a moment I just stood there on the pavement, the suitcase handle dangling from my fingers, phone to my ear, trying to understand how those words could be true.

The journey from West Acton to Waterloo was the worst tube ride of my life. I've never felt as alone as I did then. So helpless. Just me, my suitcase, and a carriage-load of regret. Two teenagers in tracksuits stared at me as I cried through the tunnels.

This South Western train isn't much better. I'm stuck on a busy carriage full of loud, talkative faces with an hour to go and no idea what to do. Help me, Sammyboys.

***

Dad tried to keep you alive before the emergency services arrived. I want you to know that. He listened to a paramedic over the phone as they instructed him on how to perform CPR. He's a superhero. Mum, too, doing everything she could, stroking your forehead like you'd asked her to in your final moments. Saying you wouldn't die. You fought and fought, didn't you? I'm sure of it. You didn't want to go.

You had a long bucket list full of items to tick off. You wanted to go on one last long-haul holiday, to the Land of the Rising Sun, while you still had the strength to travel. You wanted to lose your V plate – sorry, but I said we'd be honest with each other, didn't I? You wanted to buy more ornaments and souvenirs for your shelves. You wanted to eat more Activia yoghurt with berries, and eggs and soldiers in the morning. You wanted to live, but your body couldn't fight the pain any longer.

You don't have to worry about pain anymore. You're at peace now. You conquered Duchenne Muscular Dystrophy and squeezed that cruel, difficult-to-read disease into nothing. You never let DMD define you. You never let your adversities get in the way of your achievements. Well done, you. Top, top marks.

You know, I'll show you off to everyone. I'll be the world's best disciple. Least I can do. I'll go to the Scottish Highlands and climb Ben Nevis with Dad for his birthday. He'd love that, wouldn't he? The Airbnb we booked for him looks amazing – garden view of the Grampians. Another cracking idea from you. You're such a considerate person – I say *are* because I'm unsure if I'm ready to start writing about you in the past tense. Maybe I already have; I don't know. Whatever comes out, I'm popping it down in my Notes app – just like you did with all your lists. No filter.

I want to look at your cherished lists soon. Will you let me look at your phone when the time's right? You'd probably say something like, *Phone's all yours now, Brother Jack. Keep it. I don't need it anymore, do I?* You were always such a generous sod.

I never thought about what I said when speaking to you in person. I always felt so comfortable with you in a way I don't with anyone else. I'm an introvert, always awkward in my own skin, but with you my true self came out, in abundance.

The silliness, the laughs, the tears, the anger, the tiredness, you saw it all. Maybe Agathe does too. I like to think my fiancée knows the real me.

Your cards and gifts were the bee's knees. We were about to start planning what to get Mum for her birthday. I'll think of something special that reminds her of you. Ben Nevis will be great for Dad. Sounds like we're giving him the mountain itself. Imagine that. *Here you go, Dad. Here's Ben Nevis, tallest mountain in the UK!* He probably deserves a mountain, to be fair. As do all the Duchenne dads, and mums, and siblings. We all deserve a bloody mountain.

***

Ten-thirty. I'm arriving in Beastly Eastleigh. I came as quickly as I could. Hope you know that. I'm seeing you in a few minutes. Hold on. I'm coming to hold your hand – well,

I'd like to think I would, but it'd be weird going into your bedroom and you being there in your bed, dead. Yikes. That sounds dark. It isn't dark, though. I mean, it might be dark in your bedroom. Not sure if the lights will be on. Who knows? But this isn't dark. This is no horror movie. You're here with me, Sam. I know you are.

I'll try to hold your hand. I want to. When we were younger, we used to be so affectionate. Did Mum ever tell you that I always used to hug and squeeze you and call you a *chubby boy*? Not that you were large for a baby; you just had a lot of baby squidge, and Jacko liked Samo's baby squidge.

That sounds weird. Anyway, you're my best friend, Sam. You're still going to be my best man next year. And I'm expecting a kick-ass speech. Did you plan anything for it? Any jokes? Props? Quirky anecdotes? You always liked to be so prepared, didn't you?

Oh, before I forget, Agathe had a strange dream the other night. A premonition. She dreamt there was a framed photo of you on a table while we were saying our vows. Spooky, right? Like she knew you wouldn't be there in person.

I was sure you'd be there. I anted you to live forever.

***

Walking over the bridge now. I'm meeting Dad at The Hub, our beloved sports centre, where we used to play table tennis back in the day. When you could stand tall in your KAFOs – your transformer legs – and hit a ball with power and precision.

Dad wants to meet me there. I guess because it reminds him of you. He's not left the house since you took your last breath. I don't think anyone has. Except Megan. Her parents picked her up not long ago. It was too much for her being in the house where her boyfriend had just died. I'm glad she's with her family now.

Nearly Hub-bound, Sam. Should be able to see Dad walking towards me any second. I don't know what I'll say to him. Don't know what he'll say to me. I'm glad he's getting some fresh air.

Our family and their need for fresh air, hey? Remember Mum's wide-open windows in the bathroom? To aerate and keep the mould away. It was always so cold going into that icebox!

See you soon, Sam. I love you.

2AM

You've given me some of your strength, Sam. I'm sure of it. I'll take care of everything, don't you worry. I got this. Your funeral, the coroner's reports, whatever else needs doing – I'll handle it all.

I'm not wasting time. I'll use this superhuman strength of yours to write your eulogy – or *you*logy. Right now, lying in my old bed. I'll get the ball rolling and work through this to-do list.

It's two in the morning. I can't sleep. Don't think I will tonight.

The police, ambulances, and even a helicopter ambulance have all left – I knew you'd go out with a bang! – and so have you. I watched them zip you up. Sorry – but that's what happened. You left the house in a white body bag. I had to be there. I couldn't let you lie alone while night-time strangers took you away. It would've been degrading.

The Parents couldn't watch, which was, of course, understandable. They saw your face turn grey and your tongue flop out. I wish I could've taken this image away from them, especially for Mum – seeing you come into this world and then watching you leave it. I can't even⋯ They stayed downstairs in the living room, holding each other's hand, catching their helpless reflections blur in the black windows, realising that their lives were about to change forever. I hugged you and kissed your forehead, speaking to you like you were still alive. You looked so handsome: your thick, curly hair perfectly styled, your beard full and strong, your face radiating a calm confidence.

Is it odd that I took a photo of you, after wiping away a bit of eye bogie from the corner of your eye, seconds before the grim reapers surrounded you in darkness? Maybe. But in that moment, it felt entirely appropriate.

First thing I noticed was your smile – and that leg brace I'll never forgive myself for putting you in, but that's a story for another day.

You looked content with your short, sweet life. *Job well done.* Although your muscles were weakening day by day, you were remarkably able for someone with your condition. Thanks to your steroids or your stubbornness. Or a bitta both. Who knows? But you made sure to savour your twenty-six years on Earth.

You tasted what it was like to have a girlfriend; one that adored you. You had a job that you cared about, where you felt valued. You had a wholesome number of friends – more than I have or ever will. We liked to keep score, didn't we? You had parents who loved you, and a brother who was obsessed with you. I saw your cheeky smile and you told me not to worry.

Take your antidepressants, do your counselling, learn to love your neurodiverse self, get married to Agathe, go on an African honeymoon, and write a book about me if you must. Do whatever you need to do. Look after yourself, Brother Jack. And take some of my strength. I don't need it. I won't be walloping Duchenne anymore, will I?

Use the strength. Imagine it's spinach and you're Popeye. Don't let the spinach go to waste. Especially in the days ahead when you'll feel down in the dumps. It'll help. You'll see. Everything will be fine and dandy. I promise.

I hope so, Sam. There has to be hope, even when everything feels like nothing.

***

Your bed's empty, which is weird. What's even weirder is that I've put your wheelchair in my bedroom for company. I can reach out and feel its familiar parts from my bed, tracing the worn areas on your armrests where your elbows used to rest.

It's a tight squeeze; I have to jump over your chair to exit the room, but I don't mind. I've grown accustomed to living with that chunky obstacle. With your chair next to my bed, it's almost like you're here – like when we'd play FIFA for hours on end on my tiny TV. Those were the days.

Hope you don't mind me moving the chair. You weren't the biggest fan of people touching it – moving the headrest, fiddling with the buttons. It was part of you. Your extended body. It must've been frustrating having people interfere with it all the time.

I'm sorry for resting my feet on the framework, when we watched TV in the living room, for instance. I shouldn't have treated it like furniture. I guess I just wanted to lean on you and feel that brotherly connection.

When steering your chair to my room, I tried to not bash it into any of the woodwork. Didn't want to deepen the chips in the corners of the walls or add any new ones – we have enough of them already. I led it from your room into mine with care, like it was royalty – your mobile throne.

Wish me luck with your *you*logy, Sam. Writing about you – and to you – is all I can think about doing.

REMAINS

MONDAY 11 MARCH

Sammyboys. It's been over a week since you left us. The shock still remains. How does it feel on the other side? Do you miss living and breathing? That was a dumb question, sorry. Of course you do. I won't write rubbish like that again. I'm still working out how to communicate with you.

I wish I'd written to you more often, but I didn't feel the need. Instead, I've been talking to you out loud, like a nutcase. Like those wandering souls in Beastly Eastleigh, muttering to themselves. Like that Hagrid-lookalike with the shopping trolley and bandaged legs. Poor guy. We'd always smile at each other whenever we saw him, as if we'd spotted a celebrity. We'd say something like, *legs*, then giggle like naughty children. We could be cruel little snipes at times, couldn't we?

At random points in the day, I'll look to the side, as if you're cruising beside me. I'll say your name, ask you questions, share what I'm doing. You never reply, but that's how the cookie crumbles. When people look at me funny, I just smile until they look away, like how I used to when people stared at you in your chair. Maybe it's passive-aggressive. Oh well. I also talk to you in my head; that's probably more socially acceptable. But I prefer speaking out loud.

You're my shoulder angel. I'm always turning to you for advice.

'What photos should we use for the visual tribute, Sam?'

'What about the charities for the donations, Sam?'

'What song should we open on, Sam?'

'What about the closing song, Sam, when everyone walks out, and me, Mum, and Dad watch you get lowered into the darkness?'

'How do I do this, Sam?'

'Sam?'

***

I've been handling your afterlife admin – bank accounts, subscriptions, death certificates etc. 'Tell Us Once' is a lie, by the way; I've told the world a thousand times that you be gone now. But we're doing this together, aren't we? The Waddington Brothers, rolling up our sleeves, taking the weight off Mum and Dad's shoulders. What gents!

If our lives were switched and I'd been the one to inherit the DMD genes from Mum, you'd be on it like a car bonnet, wouldn't you? Master funeral planner, writing the best *you*logy – *me*logy? – for your big bro. Taking the reins. You were strong like that. Sorting out your care plans, keeping up to date with your meds, noting down all your hospital appointments. You had it covered.

I looked at your lists on your new iPhone – the one you bought just a week before you passed – before I finally returned it to the Apple store in Southampton. Just your luck, hey! It took an age to transfer everything across to my iCloud; you have so many photos and notes and whatnot. But I'm glad I did it. I made an album with every photo I could find of you, so you can't disappear. *Sam's Photos*. I scroll through it often. I like seeing your eyes open and mouth beaming. I like you alive, engaging in all sorts of physical activities: swimming in the sea, riding your trike around Beastly Eastleigh, zip-lining through a North American forest. Giving Duchenne the middle finger.

Those lists in your Notes app, though – wow, they're something else. Your weekly care rotas and tablet timelines never fail to cheer me up. So much detail, so much assertiveness. You managed everything so well. The older you got, the more there was to keep track of, but it didn't faze you. You simply logged it in your phone or diary, never missing a beat.

I'm trying to follow in your footsteps. Funeral planning and all the unavoidable adminy things have given me a strange kind of focus. They're helping me through these difficult days, one phone call and email at a time. That's the only way I can manage. I know it wasn't your fault you had to go – screw you, Douchebag Duchenne – but I wish you were still here. Physically, I mean – your flesh and bones, that bushy meathead, your cheeky grin. The way your limbs folded perfectly in your chair. You always had a way of helping me navigate through the rough patches. Your presence was enough.

Maybe you're still here, invisible and on my shoulder. Parked in your chair, tiny and intricate like a Warhammer figurine. Looking up at my worried face every now and then, overseeing everything in front of me, checking it's all in place, giving me a second opinion, feeding me spinach.

Sorry. That was a weak analogy. I don't even like Warhammer. And the spinach? Oh lord. I can do better. Gimmie time. Your invisibleness confuses me.

BIRTHDAY BOY

TUESDAY 12 MARCH

Happy Birthday, my little bro. I've probably said that at least fifty times today. It was the first thing that came out of my mouth when I woke up. I opened my sleep-deprived eyes, remembered you weren't here anymore, felt a sting in my chest, and whispered, 'Happy Birthday.' Then I cried.

We went to Hilly Williers Garden Centre for an afternoon tea to celebrate your big twenty-seventh. Granny, Auntie Carolyn, and Uncle Roger joined the three Waddington's – a solid team line up, I'm sure you'd agree. Granny, now in her mid-nineties, rarely gets out these days, so having her with us felt like a real treat.

Arranging the do was strange; it felt wrong phoning up and not asking for a wheelchair space. I didn't even mention you to the girl on the phone. But we had to do something. Staying at home and dwelling on your absence all day long wasn't an option. You always enjoyed a meal out, so we did it in the birthday boy's honour.

You didn't quite make it to the party Megan had planned, bless her, which was supposed to be this afternoon. Everyone was looking forward to it – especially you. It would've been an absolute blast. The people, the food, the twenty-two-hour party playlist you got carried away with making. Yes, you didn't want to miss out on any of your favourite bangers, so you crammed them all in. *Party Playlist*: three-hundred-and-thirty-two Sammyboy songs, from 'Love Shack' by The B-52's to 'Love Train' by The O'Jays. So much love, so much cheese. Just what you liked.

While an afternoon tea at Hilly Williers isn't quite the same as a big birthday bash with all your friends and family, it felt necessary. I took your framed graduation photo and placed it at one end of the table so we could all see it – like you were there with us, serviette tucked into the neck of your jumper, knife and fork at the ready, licking your lips while I plated up a carbolicious feast for you. It reminded me of Agathe's photo-at-the-wedding dream. I kept smiling at you as I tucked into sandwiches and scones. Super proud of my little bro for earning his Journalism degree, passing with flying colours, despite the teachers who once doubted you'd ever catch up with your peers.

Back at Upham Primary School, before any of us knew about Duchenne, you could still walk – a bit wobbly at times but always picking yourself up after a fall. Could this unsteady kid really compete, really succeed, among the steady walkers? Did he need a special school? Somewhere he'd 'fit in'? Nope nope, nope, you stomped. As the years went on and your legs weakened – finally giving up around twelve, when the wheelchair became permanent – you just kept going. You pushed your wheels through a world not built for wheelchair boys. Through mainstream education. Through every assumption about what you could or couldn't do. And you smashed it.

We even raised a toast to you at one point, agreeing how handsome you looked in your graduation garms. The sun shone on your tanned face, your beard was on point, and you suited those bizarre square hats graduates have to wear. You always looked good in a hat, whether it be a cap or a beanie – unlike me, who looks like someone you'd want to avoid. Maybe it's my head shape. I don't know.

I took a trip to the accessible toilet at Hilly Williers. Bit cheeky, I know, but I had my reasons. And there were no other wheelchair folk – or *bum-bounds*, as you liked to call them – around. I imagined we were there together, carer-brother and caree-brother. I held the door open for your ghostly self to slip in, then we went about our business.

Remember how we used this loo a couple of years ago when we came here for Mother's Day? It hasn't changed: still nice and roomy, no dodgy smells anywhere. Clean as a whistle. We loved rating accessible toilets – size, manoeuvrability, aesthetics, hygiene, etc.

In our early teens, before we knew any better, we also enjoyed throwing wet tissue balls at toilet walls. Especially in the Swan Centre bog in Beastly Eastleigh. The sound of soggy paper smacking the tiles never failed to make us laugh. But we always cleaned up afterwards; we were polite little Hampshire boys really. We shared plenty of laughs in those loos. I'll miss our toilet escapades, Sam.

Speaking of toilets, sorry for all the times I had a wee or number two while you were using your Urisack. That was inconsiderate of me. You'd always joke and say something like, 'I don't think other brothers' poo or wee in front of each other like this,' and you were right. They probably didn't. But we were The Waddington Brothers, and we did things differently. I've done many things that would make most older brothers cringe – trimming your toenails, shaving your pubes, some other things I'd rather not put down in words. We had a unique kind of brother bond. So when I handed you your Urisack and wet wipes – because the toilet and sink weren't exactly 'accessible' – I spotted an empty loo and thought, why not kill two birds with one stone? Why wait until after my brother's finished? So we ended up peeing side by side.

I guess I was subconsciously trying to put us at the same level, to make you feel more comfortable. I felt bad for you having to pee in front of people, so I figured it'd be more dignified if we both went at the same time. You pee; I pee – no embarrassment then. Although, having me empty my bladder while you were trying to empty yours probably made it worse. In hindsight, I could've just stood outside, like your actual carers – waiting by the closed door like a loyal dog – and only re-entered when you yelled you were done.

About that party, though. Your funeral will be the party you couldn't quite have. I'll make sure of it. I'll sort out the music, using your exhausted *Party Playlist* – I foresee this taking an eternity. Everyone you wanted there will be invited. You made a list of partygoers for Megan, saved in your Notes app: *The Definitelys*. I'll invite them all. It'll be a good old Swadders send-off.

Twenty-seven, Sam! You were nearly part of the Twenty-seven Club. Alongside troubled souls like Amy Winehouse and the soul-selling, devil-dealing blues guitarist Robert Johnson. Maybe not the best company. Perhaps it's a blessing in disguise you didn't quite make it to twenty-seven.

I don't mean it like that. I wanted you to be around forever, like I said. I wanted you to outlive me. To be an old man, despite Dooshy the Muscle Thief not allowing it. I wanted to see you with grey hair and wrinkled skin, living off your pension and telling your grandchildren stories about when you were younger.

I wanted you to look like your self-portrait on the ageing photo booth app you were obsessed with. What was it called? I can't check – I don't have your phone anymore. But you couldn't get enough of that app, especially the gender-swap feature. You'd send me so many of those ridiculous pictures. You thought I'd find them funny, which I did. Remember when you sent me an edited photo of every candidate in an old series of *The Apprentice*? The men had long, flowing hair and lipstick; the women had short hair and stubble. So daft. So you.

I'll miss getting spammed by you, Green Eggs and Spam. And I'll miss spamming you with phone calls and general silliness. And last but not least, I'll miss doing a number two in front of you.

I need to grow up.

WEDNESDAY 13 MARCH

It's six in the evening, and I'm lying in bed. In my old bedroom. I'm staying here for a while; the house I grew up in. The house you smiled your last smile in.

12 Sidders, as you liked to call it: a two-storey house tucked away in the comfort of a Hampshire cul-de-sac, pimped out with a built-in lift, a walk-in shower, and a street-to-entrance-to-garden ramp that wraps around the building like a moat. A home The Parents lovingly adapted for you, so you could access it. I'm sure you felt at home here, even if you wanted, eventually, to move out and into a place of your own. One of your life targets: to live independently. Like other people your age do.

Work's a thing of the past now. I haven't been back to Billy Bobs (we'll call the school that because why the hell not) since you left. Understandable, right? I couldn't think of anything worse. Herds of hyper children with wannabe roadman accents. Adults in suits and lanyards and leather shoes. Me – Mr. Waddington, the art teacher – pretending to have my shit together while lecturing bored teenagers on tonal variation, when all I want to do is scream like Edvard Munch and say how rubbish life is.

'Don't rush to grow up, kids. Life has a way of throwing a lot of shit at you. It's overrated. Enjoy your youth while you have it.'

Sorry, Sam, I'm in a mood.

My Angel Agathe's been staying here at 12 Sidders. She's been a gem. I need to remember this, especially when we're at each other's throats over trivial nonsense. We're both fiery, and I'm terrible with conflict. I say I hate getting into rows, but part of me thinks my wired-up ADHD head welcomes the adrenaline rush that comes with bickering. Unable to pause and reflect, I often lash out in defence and say hurtful things I instantly regret, like that Agathe's privileged Parisian upbringing makes her a bit of a brat, or how her frowning and smoking will turn her wrinkly. Got to cut that out, Sam. She's not my emotional punching bag. Yes, she can be snappy and moody and blunt and enjoys a good eye roll – like me – but she's a good egg. A good œuf.

She left for London this morning – couldn't afford to miss more work. She asked if it was ok. I said, 'Of course, mon ange,' although it wasn't easy. Having her by my side softens the pain. She's done so much for me and The Parents. Comforting us, making teas and coffee. Just being an all-around stellar human being. But I also don't want her being in the company of three weeping Waddingtons every minute of every day. She already lives with one and that's more than enough. I'm happy she's going back to the Big Smoke solo.

My old, boxy bedroom here at 12 Sidders is one of the smallest in the house. Funny how it used to be yours when you were younger, pre-diagnosis, pre-legs not working, pre-not needing space for a wheelchair, hoist, and a profiling bed. Now you have the biggest and baddest bedroom, which used to be mine. We did a swapsie, didn't we? Musical chairs but with rooms.

Our home has undergone quite the transformation since we moved in 2005. I suppose having the biggest bedroom's one perk of having a physical disability. And you had the better window view. I was always jealous of your view of the garden. All the little songbirds flittering about the magnolia tree. Beautiful. You even had starlings nesting directly above you in the loft. You could see them dart in and out of the gutter, and hear their squeaky, electronic sounds. Maybe they felt at home with your beeping hoist and chair...

My view up in London isn't that bad. I still see birds and trees and the odd fox. But you had a bloody aviary. And to observe it, all you had to do was tilt your head to the right, towards the window, while resting in your bed.

I've been lying in your bed a lot, imagining what it was like for you, what it was like *being* you. You spent a lot of time there. Your care routines took longer the older you got, the slower your body became. The less able you became. There were a lot more things you had to do before getting in and out of bed. More things that had to be put on you. Braces to keep your trousers from slipping down in your chair. Blue tape on your nose to stop your nightly breathing machine mask from causing sores. You had to spend an extra thirty minutes in bed on Sunday mornings, keeping still, waiting for your weekly risedronate tablet to do its thing, to keep your bones in check. Transferring you from your chair to your bed and getting changed took a lot longer too, especially during the recovery of your broken leg: your early Christmas present from me. I'm sorry for the pain it caused. I should've been more careful. You were such a fragile thing. It's hard to go into detail about it right now, but I will. Soon. I can't keep beating myself up.

I like horizontalising myself in your bed. Your musty smell's still there, just about, on your cushion. The one with the pug faces dotted all over the cover – what was it with your pug obsession? You couldn't get enough of those little, deformed dogs. Maybe you related to them because they were also disabled? Did that have anything to do with it?

Probably not. You probably just appreciated their squished-in faces and large, beetle-like eyes.

Do you mind if I take the cushion cover back to London? So I can have a bit of your scent with me. It was the last thing your head touched before you sealed your eyelids. It still has sweat stains on it. Your body drained itself. Slowly, throughout the day. Sweat, urine, and tears. That must've been horrible. But we don't have to speak about that leaky mess; it wasn't a pleasant experience. Maybe I should just leave the cushion cover here...

I guess you got used to it: year after year, spending longer than most on your mattress. I mean, technically you've been living with your disability longer than without it. You were only able-bodied for twelve or so years – I need to stop using the term *able-bodied*. You were able. So able. More able than a lot of able-bodied people.

But I can't help feeling bad about how you couldn't move position in your bed at night. Like I'm doing now, as I write this on my phone. Twisting and shuffling, resting on my side, bending my legs, stretching them. Doing whatever the hell I feel like doing with my body. You didn't have that luxury. You had to lie still, in one position, with your football-patterned night splints on, and your big white cushion underneath your legs, which locked them in place. You stayed like this until you woke up: legs slightly arched, socks over feet, splints over socks, jim-jams over splints. Your legs had no space to breathe – a case for serious toe jam. But you needed to sleep like that as it improved your sleep posture and spinal alignment. It stopped your lower back from being in pain.

I scratched my leg while writing the previous sentence. Right at the bottom, near my cracked heel. You wouldn't have been able to do that. I hate that you had to live the way you did. It wasn't fair. I know you never complained about it to me. To Mum or Dad, either. But it must've been hard. I would've loved for you to be able to jump out of your bed whenever you wanted to, like I'll be doing later, to go to the bathroom and brush my pearly whites. An indulgence I take for granted every single day.

I know I'm not meant to be thinking about all the things you couldn't do or achieve in your life. Instead, I should be focussing on the things you *could* do. That's the advice I'm getting online, anyway. I'm stuck on how to write your *you*logy; I'm getting writer's block. I want to do it well and show you off, like I said earlier. Good old Google's telling me to focus on the positives. All the impressive things you've done in your life. And I *will* be doing this. A lot more of this. But it's hard to do it all the time. And this isn't the *you*logy. This is me and you. Our conversations.

I'm also extremely empathetic, as I'm sure you're aware. I just can't help but feel sorry for people. I feel sorry for you because you're disabled and myself because I'm not. I don't know if that makes sense. Can you even feel sorry for yourself for *not* being disabled? I sort of feel like it at times. I wish I didn't have the burden of privilege and the tormenting guilt that comes with being the 'better-off' sibling. Why should I be allowed to run around and enjoy myself? Why should I be allowed to move and stretch and scratch my leg in bed and piss and shit and shave without needing assistance? I should be helping out my unfortunate frère who's glued to a wheelchair. I shouldn't be happy.

I don't know what I'm getting at here, Sam. I'm rambling. But I know I need to take Google's guidance and use it on myself: focus on the positives. Jack's positives. It's a challenging ask when I'm a grieving mess like this. But noticing one little highlight each day's a start, right?

26

THURSDAY 14 MARCH

Good evening, Mr. Sam.

Mr. Bean's Teddy has been keeping my head and cushion company for the last week or so. I sleep next to him, like I'm a toddler again. He was the last soft toy you treated yourself to – an early birthday present to yourself. You sent me a photo of him on WhatsApp, captioned *BEAN*. Sunday, 25th February, 3:56 PM – your final message to me.

You were so proud of your purchase. And you knew I'd appreciate it too. We thought highly of Mr. Bean and his knitted friend.

Remember when we used to watch the original *Mr. Bean* on VHS at Grandma's old house in Wareham? We loved seeing his silly facial expressions when getting into everyday predicaments. We liked to mimic him and see who could do the best impersonation. We also pitied the child trapped in a grown-up's body.

It made me chuckle how you said you felt uncomfortable buying Teddy – going up to the cashier in Clinton Cards in Beastly Eastleigh, holding a Ty bear like a guilty pleasure.

I still have the £9.99 price tag attached to his head – feels wrong to remove it now. I want to keep everything of yours how you left it.

Hope you don't mind me pinching Teddy from your room. It was the last photo you sent to me; it felt right, like you wanted me to have it. I nearly bought the bear in Harrods just a couple of days before you did, funnily enough. Great minds think alike, hey? Well, now I don't have to buy it. I can hold onto yours.

I'll never get rid of Teddy. His value has skyrocketed since you left. He's now worth far more than £9.99. Pour toi, he was one of your hundreds of toys and morsels of memorabilia. Pour moi, he's part of you – one of the most precious things I own.

Bedtime now. My eyelids are drooping. I'm listening to Rachmaninov on Spotify. The sound of the piano's making me sleepy.

Night, Sammy.

Night, Teddy.

Night, Rachmaninov.

DEATH ADMIN

FRIDAY 29 MARCH

Time's been breaking the speed limits, Sam. It's nearly April. I feel like you're turning into a memory, and it's tough to stomach. To cope, I'm keeping myself busy with the funeral party and everything in between. It's a full-time job.

You'd be proud of me – I'm on it twenty-four-seven, like a machine. I've stuck to my word and stayed super organised. My current mission: to complete your *you*logy. Vicky – a lovely woman of celebrant ilk who visited us at 12 Sidders earlier today – has given me until Sunday to email it to her. Then she'll review it and print it out, ready for the big ceremony next week – April 4th, Sam. It's happening.

I still talk to you out loud. Sometimes you're a miniature Sammy on my shoulder, like one of the ornaments on your souvenir shelf. Other times, you hover beside me in your chair – invisible but present. I can take you anywhere now. No need for ramps, door widths, or drop-down curbs. No more phone calls. Just me and you, on demand.

Remember how it used to take us a hot, sweaty eternity to navigate through train stations, looking for step-free platforms and lifts – which, of course, often weren't in operation. People would stare at us like we were aliens. Two hairy brothers, one in a wheelchair, the other looking skinny and lost. I always made sure to stare back at them: the clueless starers. Sometimes I'd mutter things under my breath like, 'Haven't you ever seen a wheelchair before?' 'Yes, it's a wheelchair; lucky you're not in one, mate,' or, one I borrowed from Mum – an old Trinidadian saying she used when growing up in the Caribbean – 'Hey goblin, you gotta staring problim?' You know the one, Sam. Got to love our island mama – born and raised there, like her dad and grandad before her. Trini 2 De Bone.

No more of those snarky comments, though. No more scrutinising eyes from strangers. No more feeling like you're being watched. Now you can drift beside me like you're some sort of Jedi spirit. Or a sidecar to my motorbike. An invisible friend.

Ergh – a memory, a shelf souvenir, a Warhammer figurine, a Jedi spirit, a sidecar, and now an invisible friend. I'm coming up with some wild metaphors for you, desperately trying to describe what you are now. Even though I know you're not here.

I know it's just me, pretend-talking to you. If only you could be back in your chair, leaning your meathead against the sweaty headrest, resting your feet on the dirty footplates covered in fallen debris from mealtimes. Bliss.

I'd give anything to be stranded on the middle platform at Beastly Eastleigh train station on a rainy winter night because the lift was out of order again.

Remember that dreadful journey a few years back? How we got off at Beastly Eastleigh, after our night out seeing a Bee Gees tribute act in Southampton, ready for our short walk to 12 Sidders, but couldn't get across to street level? We had to use our initiative and board another train, this time to Winchester, where there *was* a working lift. Then, like two washed-up Gibbs, we had to find a taxi company that actually had accessible taxis operating that feverish Saturday night – not easy – and wait outside the station for twenty minutes in the cold – you shivering because you didn't have a blanket, me rubbing your legs to keep them warm – until an accessible taxi finally picked us up and drove us home.

Deep breath.

At 12 Sidders, we went upstairs – you via lift, me via steps – then I hoisted you into bed and got you changed into your jim-jams.

Another deep breath.

'See you in the morning, Sam.'

'Thanks, Jack. You too.'

'Bloody lifts, hey!'

'Bloody lifts.'

We didn't get to sleep until around one in the morning. Heads pounding, ears still ringing with Bee Gees falsetto.

Bring back those headaches.

J A C C I D E N T

CONFESSION

I think I'm ready to talk about your broken leg now.

People say that it wasn't my fault: what happened last Christmas Eve, in your bedroom, after your shower. They say it could've happened to anyone. Any family member, any carer. I've tried a thousand times to repeat those words to myself like a spell, but it doesn't help. I don't believe them. You've only ever broken your leg while in my care, Sam. Not just once, but twice. Once in Wales – that's another story – and then at 12 Sidders, last year. Both times, I was meant to be looking after you.

I said that I wouldn't be feeling remorseful and confessing, but minds change. The peg-related events scarred me big time. I think I need to acknowledge them. And I need forgiveness. From you, my godly brother. For my bones are troubled, as yours once were.

It *was* my fault. Last Christmas. I was clumsy, like I always am. Clumsy Jack, breaking phones, crockery, cameras, and now his disabled brother's left leg. Jaccidents. Yes, I can be careful. I've always told you how I'd never let you get hurt. That you could trust me. But I overestimated myself. I ignored my innate clumsiness. It comes in waves – when I'm not thinking straight or getting overexcited. When my mask's off.

I should've remembered that your bones were weaker, that you'd lost a lot of strength in the last years of your life. Dooshy had gradually taken away your mobility and muscle mass. By your mid-twenties, you needed your ventilator more often, struggled to sit up, to lift your hands. You couldn't give me a high five or hold a cup of tea. I should've remembered all that. I shouldn't have pulled you up from the bed the way I did. The way I'd been doing for years and years. So firmly. So assuredly.

Since your teens, I've pulled you up by the arm. One quick motion, like yanking up a heavy leaver. Gritting my teeth, pulling my body back. Maybe to show off, to prove I was strong. Maybe I was re-enacting footballers pulling up teammates, so we could spend some quality time together. But all your weight was lifted by my slim but willing arm.

You slipped off the bed, naked, onto the laminate floor. Less than a metre, but it must've hurt. Your bed was higher than most, raised after showers for easier care. You didn't wince or cry. You just lay there on your back, helpless.

The image poisons my mind. I have flashbacks of it. You looked like a baby. Naked, still, not able to move.

I panicked, trying to keep quiet so Mum and Dad wouldn't hear – especially Mum as she'd lose her shit, which she did when she found out. Rightly so. She knew the consequences. The discomfort it would cause.

I thought about how I could get the sling under you and hoist you back onto the bed. But you insisted you couldn't move.

'Too painful. I've broken it.'

'No, Sam, you can't have.'

'It's broken. Call the ambulance. Please, Jack.'

I gulped. I didn't want to admit it, but you were right. You knew your body.

'Shit, Sam. I'm sorry. Fuck.'

'It's ok. Accidents happen.' You forced a smile through gritted teeth.

'Are you sure it's broken? Not just bruised?'

'No, it's broken. I know what it feels like.'

'Shit... Right, let me put a cushion under your head.'

Your head was cornered awkwardly against the bottom of the chest of drawers and the wooden floor.

'Ok. But do it carefully.'

I lifted your head with one hand and slid a cushion from your bed under it with the other. You winced as I did this. 'Is that better?'

'Kind of. Thanks.'

'I'll ring the ambulance.'

'Thanks. You should tell Mum and Dad too.'

I gulped again. 'I know. I will.'

***

I'm so sorry, Sam. For that unnecessary obstacle. All the difficulties it caused you, Mum and Dad, your carers, Megan, work. Everyone. I'm sorry for making you wear a permanent leg splint and be on morphine for the last couple of months of your life. You died wearing that splint. That detail kills me.

You know, part of me feels like I killed you. I know you'd be the first to tell me that's absurd, but the shame lingers. Your last few months on earth shouldn't have been spent in pain with a fractured leg. Maybe it weakened your body, your spirit, your fight. Maybe that's why you left a mere seventy-one days later. Too much for you to bear. It made everything so much more difficult. Meeting up with Megan, for instance. You'd planned to stay at a hotel with her on New Year's Eve, so you could pop that cherry of yours, and that never happened. Intimacy for wheelchair users was tough enough, let alone with a broken leg. I feel responsible for that.

If I knew I was going to lose you for good, I would've been so bloody careful with you. I would've treated you like a king, doing everything you wanted – or needed – me to do.

All the things I complained about doing over the years. I would've lovingly sprinkled seeds and placed raspberries onto your Activia pots and made you eggs and soldiers in the morning without saying how I felt marmite on toast would've sufficed for breakybobs. I would've given you endless cups of water with your Movicol while you desperately tried to relieve your bowels without saying how I thought they wouldn't help. I would've picked up the bottles of shampoo or shower gel you'd accidentally dropped in the shower without sighing and muttering how you could've been more careful. If you'd asked me to, I would've run downstairs and made you a hot water bottle without question. No whining. I would've just done it.

It'll take me a long time to forgive myself for what happened last Christmas. That's why I need forgiveness from you first – I know that you forgave me already, in person, multiple times, and I appreciate that, but I need to hear it again, from your floaty, invisible self. Then I can follow in your footsteps.

Great bloody timing too, hey? Day before Christmas. Your favourite time of the year – when the family can get together and enjoy themselves. And after one of the best Christmas Eve Eves we'd ever had, watching Beastly Eastleigh FC play at the Silverlake Stadium; your actual Christmas present from me, not the leg break.

***

I was so excited to give you the printed-out tickets. We'd always wanted to go to our local club's ground, but we never got around to it. Life always getting in the way.

That day was one of the best moments of my life, Sam. Really. Me, you, and Dad, watching bang-average National

League football on an overcast Saturday afternoon. Setting up shop in one of the many accessible bays – for such a small ground, it was surprisingly disabled-friendly. Sitting next to the dad of one of the Beastly Eastleigh FC footballers, Lee Hodson – who used to be in one of my career mode teams on FIFA. We were chuffed about that. We spoke to the proud dad, commenting on how well his son was playing at right back. Using his experience to grind out a result.

Beastly Eastleigh beat Dorking Wanderers two-one that evening. We cheered like we'd been supporting The Spitfires our whole lives. We loved it and decided to follow Beastly Eastleigh FC from that moment onwards, along with our Stoke and The Arsenal. We kept analysing the line-up and talking tactics when we got home after the game. How good Paul McCallum looked – an assured striker. We also looked at the future fixtures on the club website, thinking about the home games we could potentially go to before the end of the season. It was the start of a special bond between us and our hometown club.

***

The day after Beastly Eastleigh FC won at the Silverlake Stadium was a living nightmare. Southampton General Hospital Emergency Room. The four Waddingtons lost for words. Mum and Dad looking exhausted, you in a lot of agony, and me, struck with tremendous guilt, biting my fingernails and the skin around them until they bled. I was a nervous wreck, pacing around, waiting for the nurse to see you, asking them how much longer, making a nuisance of myself. Hearing the doctor confirm that your left femur bone had cracked in half gave me a hundred bee stings. Knowing six months of your life would be unnecessarily challenging. The guilt was too much. I wanted to hit myself – and did, scratching my forehead and punching my head when no one was looking.

You caused this, Jack. Look at your poor parents. They're over sixty and they're spending Christmas at A&E. They don't deserve this. They'll have to deal with the aftermath of all this. You won't. You'll go back to London and live your life. You come home for a week, break your brother's leg, then fuck off. That was your Christmas gift to your family.

The doctor told us that you'd need either an operation or a leg splint to mend your cracked femur. Two shit solutions. Waiting for that evaluation was worse than waiting for confirmation of the bone snap. More finger biting, more clawing at my skin. I was drowning in a sea of self-loathing. On one occasion, I found blood on my finger after raking my nails across my forehead. The sting was sharp, the marks likely evident, but I welcomed that suffering; it felt like a fitting punishment.

I felt a sense of relief when we found out that you didn't need to be operated on. The dangers of an operation, knowing how brittle your bones were. How your leg would be disfigured as a result of the surgery – that's right; a scar I'd have to see for the rest of my life. A reminder of what a shit I was. And we didn't want you staying in the hospital much longer. But the feeling of relief was short-lived. They said that you'd need to be in their care and stay at Southampton General for at least two more nights. Two more nights? To put a splint on. They were having a laugh.

I asked if I could stay the night with you, so you had someone beside you on Christmas Day morning. They wouldn't allow it. Health and safety or whatever flimflam. That made me growl and clench my fists. How could they let you wake up on Christmas Day alone?

We left you in that dark, lonely ward on your favourite evening of the year. You smiled and told us it'd be ok, that you'd be fine. That you were used to hospital wards. But we knew it'd be hard for you – and harder for us, probably, without our Sam. The life of Christmas.

We drove home in the big van, Dad at the wheel, tired and bamboozled with everything, Mum just as drained beside him, and me covered in tears and snot, crying like a baby. I kept telling our mama and papa how sorry I was, and how much of a horrid brother I was. I don't think they'd ever seen me break down like that. I've always tried to act so strong in front of them. The oldest son. Someone they could be proud of. Not in that car journey home. I was a sticky mess.

I didn't sleep a wink that night. I stayed up texting you, checking in on you. Because I knew you wouldn't be sleeping well either. The drugs would need to be topped up in your body at two-hourly intervals throughout the night. I told you to try and get some sleep, even if it was only for a couple of hours between those intervals. I stayed awake, shedding tears and feeling helpless. Hoping that you were sleeping.

You texted me this at four in the morning:

I'm ok Jack. Yes, not in excruciating pain because very kind nurses regularly giving me pain relief. Ringing buzzer whenever need help. Not too frightened in safe hands.

Christmas Day arrived. The three Waddingtons came as early as they were able to. I wanted to arrive earlier than nine o'clock, but Mum and Dad were shattered and needed to eat breakfast before leaving. I said I'd get a taxi to the hospital so I could see you earlier and then meet them later at the hospital. Mum didn't like the sound of that.

'Jack, you can't get a taxi on Christmas Day. Just come with us. And eat something, please.' She was concerned as I hadn't eaten anything since pulling you off the bed the day before.

I listened, gave in, and took a bite from a banana, but the act of eating and indulging myself made me feel nauseous, so I stopped. We brought presents for you. Our attempt at bringing your favourite time of the year to you. We brought the things you'd requested from me over the phone. A peculiar but manageable selection. I remember writing the items down like nothing in the world was more important than your requests.

- *Xmas crossword book*
- *Santa hat*
- *One present (doesn't matter which one, just pick one at random)*
- *A couple of small Xmas ornaments from bedroom*
- *The photos and frame for Megan's present*

You were so positive and determined to make the best out of every situation. You wanted your new clinical surroundings to feel Christmassy. I hope they did.

Apart from a few nibbles on sandwiches and leftover snacks, I hardly ate on Christmas Day. I cared for you and Mum and Dad like an absolute robot. It was the least I could do. I summoned my reserve energy and used it up that day. I felt like one of the nurses on autopilot, rushing around, making sure our parents ate, making sure you were being looked after properly. I even helped to take you to the toilet. A number two in a hospital ward – a hullabaloo waiting to happen.

After attempting and failing to slide a flimsy cardboard bed pan underneath your bom-bom- you're one heavy boy, Sam; and it was hard to do this without hurting your leg – the nurses had to lift you in a portable hoist, so you could release your bowels in mid-air. I held the bedpan underneath you – you didn't want the nurses helping. Fair enough; I wouldn't either, if I were you.

It was a humiliating experience. The curtains were closed to create your 'private' enclosure, but nurses and patients around could hear everything. I wanted to tell everyone to bugger off out of the room and let me deal with my brother on my own. He'd appreciate more than a closed curtain. You managed to do your number two. And I managed to not get any of it on my hands. A success if you ask me, considering I had to hold your broken leg in a certain way, so it didn't cause you too much pain. Juggling the cardboard bedpan and your leg – not easy. You peed a bit on my arm – but that felt like a fair price for breaking your leg. It was probably the most makeshift toilet experience you've ever had – but we managed it. We always manage. The perfect duo.

We kept pestering the nurses and doctors to speed things up. To make their decision on the discharge, the medication, the paperwork that needed to be signed. They were doing the best they could, due to the limitations on staff during the holiday season, but we wanted out. Mum, Dad, and I were sick of Costa Coffee meals from the café near reception – the only place serving food that was open in the afternoon, it seemed. You were sick of your sorry-looking hospital meals. We wanted 12 Sidders.

Remember how we used your Notes app to explain why you needed to be discharged and go back home rather than stay another night? Here's what we crafted:

- *Sam needs a shower and can't shower here.*
- *The care at home will be more efficient – Sam will be able to use his breathing machine and go to the toilet more readily.*
- *The antibiotics and lots of water are the treatment – there's no need for Sam to stay here any longer. It's a waste of everyone's time.*
- *Sam needs to go home to adjust to his new care routines – carers need to adapt to home care as Sam will be in a leg splint for some time.*

It worked. They recognised our dissatisfaction with the level of care you were receiving. The facilities were inadequate for showering you or assisting you to the toilet with dignity. You were feeling unclean, and they could see the exhaustion and desperation etched on our faces. Your leg needed the comfort of home to heal. Keeping you at the ward for unnecessary checks and rest was pointless. They agreed to let us go on Boxing Day, but only after one more night in the ward.

Buggeration!

I was resolute about staying with you that night – your second and final evening there. I informed the nurses that you'd need someone by your side until morning to assist with your breathing machine, which you hadn't used the previous night. I mentioned that going two sleeps – or lack thereof –

without it wasn't an option, which was a slight exaggeration. I said that it could have serious repercussions for your lungs, while you looked up at them with your finest puppy-dog eyes. Knowing the nurses wouldn't want to take the risk, we had a good chance.

It did the trick; they caved in. They allowed me to stay with you for that last night to operate the ventilator, but I had to make do with a sofa chair since they couldn't provide a bed. I was already aware that a bed wasn't an option, and it didn't bother me in the slightest. I knew sleep wouldn't come, and it didn't.

I spent the entire night by your side, whispering apologies and holding your small hand. It felt so soft and warm in mine. Your fingers slender, your nails elegantly long.

Remember how we used to compare our hands? We'd agree on how yours were smooth and effeminate, like Mum's, while mine were rough and stubby, like Dad's. We were such nincompoops.

You also had a codeine drip inserted into a vein on your wrist. That image still haunts me. I've never been good with injections. But I kept holding your hand, repeating that I love you, I love you, I love you, I love you, Sam.

In the early hours of the morning, feeling the need to voice my distress, and not knowing who to talk to or who I could trust, I joined a Facebook community group for adult siblings of people with disabilities. I posted a message – along with a photo of The Waddington Brothers smiling – explaining what had happened. I felt vulnerable and in need of support. I didn't know what to expect when posting that early-morning SOS message. A few virtual hugs. Perhaps some soothing words from people in a similar situation. And

I got them. I was bombarded with over fifty messages from kind, generous siblings across the globe. Offering their support and sending me love and strength. Telling me how great of a brother I was. It was what I needed to hear in the darkness of that ward.

Thank you to all those thoughtful people. I haven't spoken to many of them since. I don't know how to. I gave a brief thank you to every one of the comments and that was that. I guess I just needed to hear that I wasn't alone.

That's why I called the Samaritans too. I wasn't suicidal, but I needed to let things off my chest. They listened and said that I wasn't to blame for the jaccident. They said I could phone them back at any time. While talking to other siblings and the Samaritans made me feel less isolated, it didn't change how terrible I felt about myself.

Spending Christmas in pain like that isn't ideal. I know how much you loved Crimbobs. Our last one together was a peculiar one, but we made sure we had some giggles.

That funny man in the bed next to you still makes me laugh. He kept requesting cream crackers and a spare sandwich in the dead of the night. He asked the nurse for movie recommendations during breakfast – he went with *Titanic* in the end, and so did you, while I sat beside you, fighting off yawns. I loved seeing how half the ward was glued to their private TV's, all watching your favourite film on Christmas Day. It seemed like the sandwich man had Alzheimer's or something. He didn't know where the hell he was or who he was. Yet his unexpected requests gave us something to chuckle about. How rude we were. Laughing at a man who had some issues. We do that a lot. We're going to hell, Sam. Maybe you're already there? Chilling in a jacuzzi cauldron.

I'm nodding off now. I'm leaving the confession booth. I apologise, ok. I never meant to hurt you. I messed up. I guess we'll talk about this again sometime. Right now, it wears me out thinking back to Christmas 2024. I feel exhausted. Sweaty on the outside, fluttering guilt butterflies on the inside. They'll disappear, eventually.

Am I forgiven, Lord Sam?

MONDAY 1 APRIL

I'm on a train heading to Beastly Eastleigh – I've been back in London for a couple of days. Mainly to pick up some more clothes and give Agathe a hug. I need to be at 12 Sidders with Mum and Dad. They're scared to be on their own in the house they saw you die in. Agathe, French and fabulous as ever, will join me there on Wednesday. Day before your funeral party.

I have a six-seater all to myself; one of the benefits of travelling in the middle of the day. I'm armed with my suitcase – the same one I took home the day you died – and a Marks & Spencer bag holding my navy-blue suit. I've only worn it once, to a friend's wedding last summer. Can you wear the same suit to a wedding and a funeral? Not sure. Feels a bit wrong, but everything feels wrong right now.

I also have a bubble-wrapped framed collage, filled with over fifty photos of you. I've only gone and made a photo collage, like the ones Grandad used to make, to showcase his family, his Waddington dynasty. I started and finished it last night. Only took me a couple of hours.

It was quite the scene. A hundred photographs I'd printed from Boots were scattered across the wooden floorboards of my flat. I cut away at them like a psychopath – your meatheads, your bodies, other people's heads and bodies – gluing them frantically to an A3 corkboard without too much regard to composition. My mission: fill the gaps. Simples. You'd have laughed at the ludicrousness of it all. The Frenchy sure did. Every now and then she'd peek into the living room, snickering.

'Having fun?'

'Yes. I'm on a roll – a bacon roll.'

'I can see, my love.'

She sometimes calls me *my love*, like you called Megan. I call her names like *sweet angel-droplet* or *my sexy, little beast* when I'm feeling cheeky. She usually enjoys it, though sometimes I think she'd prefer if I just called her *my love.*

'I'm trying to make sure I don't miss out on any of Sam's friends. Or family. I don't want to offend anyone at the funeral party. I'm going to display it there. He'll love it.'

'That's a great idea. I'm sure you won't. And I'm sure he'll love it.'

She's being extra kind to me lately. Mourning perks.

'I have five photos of him with Mum, and only three of him and Dad. Fiddlesticks!'

'Oh, Jamie won't like that.'

'No, he bloody won't!'

I can act like a real sillybilly in front of my fiancée.

'Right, gotta find a few more of Sammyboys with Jamieboys.' I rummaged through the glossy photos, panting like a dog.

Agathe raised an eyebrow at me. 'Ok, I'm going to leave you now before this gets too weird. Good luck.'

Before getting it framed, I added your name in Scrabble letters across the middle of the collage. I found the small beige pieces at my local Rymans in Ealing. I thought it was a nice touch, knowing how much you adored Scrabble.

Your collage will go in the room where the reception will be. Where people will be eating nibbles and drinking tea or coffee and thinking about you. We're having your send-off at Chesil House in Winchester. We didn't want it anywhere else, Sam. They did a great job with Grandad's funeral last year, didn't they? And it's a beautiful location, right by that glistening river. I'm sure you'd approve.

I'll gift the masterpiece to Mum and Dad. I think it'd look good above the dining room table. A comforting visual while they have their dinner. I'm going to make one for myself too – just us two. A clean white frame, hung up somewhere in my flat. Agathe won't mind. I hope not. She's allowed to put all her stuff up: fridge magnets, ornaments, plates, jugs, cosmetics, her endless Sunny Angel collection – lil naked angel figurines with mini willies and colourful headgear – as weird as they sound, they're kind of cute, Sam.

My turn now. All I have on display is my collection of tattered books on our shared bookshelf and shiny pins on my corkboard. I want your collage up on a wall somewhere, so you and your many faces can cheer me up when I'm feeling low. Maybe I can show it to my future children, whenever they arrive – I'm hoping within the next two or three years, Sam. I want to be a papa. And I want to show them Uncle Sam – not that one, although you'd look good in his blue-white-red top hat. You're going to be the best uncle ever. Kind, gentle, and supportive. Something else to tick off your bucket list.

***

I'm still on the train, sinking into the seat like a tired drunk, laptop open in front of me. I'm looking out the window, feeling a little numb, not knowing if I'll be able to manage the funeral party.

Of course I will. I just have a few pre-match nerves, that's all. At least I don't have to worry about doing a speech – Vicky the celebrant is reading your *you*logy. I wanted to say a few words, like Mum and Dad will, but I'm too shy. I get serious stage-fright, and I want the *you*logy to be read clearly, without me trembling or breaking down. I'm sure you understand. Vicky has bucket loads of experience and a super friendly face. I trust her to deliver the goods.

You're currently in a Word document by the way. The words were multiplying hammer and tongs, and it became too fiddly trying to write to you on my Notes app. I prefer Word. Cleaner layout. Lets me format the book with chapter titles. Much easier to navigate. Plus, it makes everything look all polished and professional.

A vast wetland area near Fleet is sliding past me. Waterbirds gliding through the serene lakes, like they've got all the time in the world. Lucky bastards. I just caught a glimpse of a great crested grebe, flaunting its flashy orange, white, and black ruff. Such cool birds. They remind me of Ziggy Stardust.

I think I'm going to visit this mysterious wetland centre someday, binoculars and boots in tow. Looks like a short walk from Fleet train station. I haven't been birdwatching in ages. It became my passion during lockdown, didn't it? I remember calling you at half-six one morning to tell you I was staring at a little owl perched in a tree at Regents Park – my very first wild owl sighting – and I had to share my excitement with my little bro.

Second wild owl sighting was a long-eared owl in Farlington Marshes a few years later. What a sight. I couldn't call you on that occasion because I didn't have signal at the nature reserve. I saw and heard my very first curlew that day too, with its long beak and beautiful bubbling call.

I miss the thrill of hunting for birds.

I miss telling you all about it too. Any flutter was reason enough to pick up the phone and hear your voice.

***

Random train thought: I'm sorry for all the times I got frustrated with your eating habits – I promise I'll quit confessing soon. Just let me get this out of my system quick.

I often found myself irritated by the way you handled your knife and fork. The mess you made when you ate. How food slipped through your fingers when you tried to cut or pick something up, like the cutlery was too slippery, too difficult to grip. I could manage it, and I assumed others could too. I noticed how food sometimes landed in your lap on the journey from plate to mouth. It was just too much of a challenge for you to not drop anything. Like those egg-and-spoon races we did at Upham.

I let my annoyance and disgust get the better of me. The messiness of it all. The perceived carelessness. I thought you could've concentrated more, which is bullshit, I know. You *were* concentrating. Trying so hard not to get your beard dirty, not to get your fingers in the food, not to make a blunder. But slow, deliberate movements weren't possible anymore. Yours were quick and clumsy, like sustaining control of your hands was a monumental task. You'd grimace, lift your arm, do something with your hand, like itch your beard mid-meal, then let your arm flop down like it'd given up. At the time, I didn't get that raising your arms sapped you of energy. I only saw the mess and got vexed.

Why can't my brother eat normally? Why do I have to be reminded of a toddler on a highchair when he eats? He's in his mid-twenties and he requires a kitchen roll tucked into the neck of his shirt like a bib to collect food droppings. For fuck's sake.

I felt bad for you as well as frustrated by you. I desperately wanted you to be 'normal.' I wasn't being understanding, and I'm sorry for that. For getting cranky at the things you couldn't help doing. For the judgemental eyes across the dinner table.

And it's not like I was the tidiest eater. I'm notorious for my lack of dining-table etiquette. Elbows on the table, eating with my mouth open. Ask Agathe's family. They love a good fine-dining experience at elaborate restaurants in Paris or London, when they come to visit their daughter and Baldylocks from Beastly Eastleigh. I feel so out of place eating with them. Not knowing how the hell to eat an oyster, how to retrieve meat from a lobster, or how to do something simple like eat bread before a meal. Yes, Sam – bread! I remember getting a table full of side-eyes at their holiday home in Cap Ferret when I picked up a slice of bread from the basket and spread fish pâte over it like I was making a sandwich. Apparently, you're only meant to tear off small pieces of bread and apply small portions of spread onto them. Who knew? I certainly made – and continue to make – a fool out of myself when around the Frenchies. I should've known better when directing side-eyes your way.

Part of me thinks it wasn't entirely my fault: judging you the way I did. For as long as I can remember, I've been irked seeing people make a mess. Grinds my gears. Grosses me out. I'm a clean freak; I can't stand grubbiness on people. I cringe at toddlers with food smeared over their faces – God knows what I'll be like with kids of my own. But it was worse seeing you in the act. An adult. I didn't want to have to witness it, every day, every evening. I'd step in, grab your wet wipes, and clean you because I couldn't control my discontent. I didn't even ask before wiping your hands, your chin, or changing your kitchen-roll bib. I just got up and hosed you down when I couldn't take it anymore.

You know, I think there was also a part of me that thought you probably wouldn't have wanted a big splodge of ketchup on your chin, or your thumb coated in gravy. Maybe I was trying to protect your dignity. It's harder for disabled people to stay clean. That's just the reality. It was harder for you to clean yourself. And to aerate yourself. That's why you'd smell of BO often.

I also didn't like that part of you – truth's coming out now on this South Western Railway carriage. Maybe I should only write to you on these trains from now on.

The BO irritated me. And I felt bad for Mum having to constantly wash your clothes. Especially those thick collared shirts. Again, it wasn't your fault. You couldn't help your underarms producing that much sweat. You couldn't lift your arms as easily as you once were able to do. The sun definitely didn't shine on those pits. They lived in the dark, barely seeing daylight, no chance to breathe.

I could smell the sweat when I cared for you, when I got you ready for your shower – stepping in during holidays or weekends home from London, whenever your carers weren't around. Off came your T-shirt and nosey me leant in and smelt your shadowy pits. Lifting your arm like you were a rag doll. That was wrong of me. I was too intrusive at times, bringing attention to situations you couldn't help and probably felt ashamed of. Your carers didn't treat you like that, so there was no excuse for me to do so.

But we had fun with your pits, didn't we? We gave those bad boys a whopping clean in the walk-in shower.

'Right, Sam. I'm gonna lather your sponge with soap and scrub your hairy pits like there's no tomorrow!'

You'd giggle and get all excited. 'Let's do it, Brother Jack!'

I cleaned your underarms so thoroughly they got a little red at times. That was a good sign, though. It meant the BO had gone, until tomorrow came. Sometimes I shaved your armpit hair off with your manual razor – after you gave me the nod, of course, and I applied shaving cream – to get rid of the sweaty hair so we could get right up close to the skin and clean away. To let that skin of yours breathe.

As I said, I'm a sucker for hygiene. Showering you was never a half-arsed job. I cleaned you like my existence depended on it. Sometimes, when I was pumped up, I was too hasty. But I was always efficient, ensuring there wasn't a trace of BO after your shower.

Afterward, we went back to your bedroom, where I hoisted you onto your bed, and dusted your underarms with a cloud of talcum powder – doing this always made me feel like I was preparing you for a wrestle in a ring. One at a time, I lifted your arms and attacked your pits with Dove deodorant like it was fly repellent. The Raging Bull was ready.

But you probably didn't want me making such a fuss over your pits. You knew they often smelt bad. You were embarrassed by that. I know you were. And I kept bringing your attention back to it, making you feel more embarrassed than you already did. Was that dickish of me? Probably.

Sometimes, I feel it's too late to confess to all my jaccidents. You aren't around to accept my apologies anymore. But I also feel like it's now or never. And if you're here, in spirit or God form – à la Allah, Zeus, Shiva, or whoever's on duty – then you'll hear me, and it wouldn't have been too late.

Rain's trickling over the countryside. There's a man in the distance with an umbrella and a large hound. The Hampshire houses are getting cleaned. I'm gonna give my laptop a break now, Sam – getting headachy screen eyes.

Speak soon, Sweatbox.

FUNERAL PARTY

THURSDAY 4 APRIL

Might not be able to write a lot today, Sam. I'm currently typing away on my phone next to your coffin.

We went for a plain and simple one. It's called *The Sussex*. The funeral directors at Chesil House gave us a brochure that offered a range of coffins all named after different UK counties. Slightly fucking bizarre, but anyway. I would've liked to go with a casket, but they come with a hefty price tag. The coffin you're resting in looks great. It's like you're in a treasure chest. Or Count Orlok having a nap. It has a smooth oak finish with shiny brass handles.

The room's empty. Bill Withers' 'Lovely Day' is playing in the background. Your playlist's on loop, Sam. *Sam's Reception*. I put most of your favourite songs on it – it took ages, with all your one-hit wonders, deep cuts, and random gems to sieve through. I think I did your music taste justice. Summed you up in thirty-two songs. From 'Perfect 10' by The Beautiful South to 'True Blue' by Madonna. No one's here to hear it yet. The music's just for you.

I'm sitting down in the front row. Your hidden body's a metre away from me, lying down. Fortified. I hope you aren't too squished. Do you have a soft fabric padding around you? Or a duvet-type thing beneath you? What's it like in there? Are you wearing the clothes we gave to the funeral directors? Your final outfit: black and white collared shirt, grey tracksuit bottoms, shiny black shoes? Smart-casual. And can't forget the sneaky fox brooch you wore at Grandad's funeral – because foxes were his favourite animal. You bought it just for the occasion. Your funeral charm. I'm glad you're not wearing your leg splint. Bet you were chuffed to say goodbye to that bugger.

We didn't want an open casket. One thing that me and The Parents agreed on without much discussion. We didn't want to see you in make-up and combed hair and whatever else they did to you. We felt that'd be too odd. You're still embalmed. I imagine your arms are resting on your chest and you've got that gentle grin on your face that we all know so well.

On top of The Sussex, a show-off red and white flower display screams *SAM*. Red and white – the colours of Stoke City, Arsenal, England, Southampton, and Trinidad and Tobago – technically the Socca Warriors play in red and black, but still. All your teams represented. Go football! It's a sight to behold, it really is. I can't stop staring at it. Your good friend from college, Ian, and his wife, Anna, had it made for you. They can't be here today because they're abroad, but they'll be watching the live stream from Greece – your funeral party's being streamed online, like a football match! How cool is that?

Agadoodoos is sitting beside me. I couldn't have done any of this without her. Or maybe I could have. You gave me your spinach, didn't you? I'm a warrior now – straight off the Socca Warriors' bench and into the match. And a worrier. What The Agatron's done, though, is help me to worry less. I need to give her more attention, and affection. She has this catchy tune she used to sing when she was head over heels for Jacko, 'Give her what she wants, give her what she needs; hugs and kisses, hugs and kisses.' Adorable, really.

It's the calm before the storm, Sam. Over a hundred people will be coming to fill this room in thirty minutes' time. Squeaky bum time. Feels like a pre-match warm up.

Sprinklers on the field, players out training, fans finding their seats, pumping party playlist in the background. You'd be gearing up for the occasion, clinging to your hot chocolate, concentration face at the ready.

It's 'Moving on Up' by M People now. I can picture you busting a move to these beats in your new wooden pad. Giving your body a good old groove.

***

Ok, I think my fidgety fingers need a break from typing – I'm so bloody nervous. Time to go downstairs and get ready to greet everyone and receive their condolences. Your socially awkward brother playing host – no idea how I'll manage it. I'll put on a brave face and go into teacher mode. Mr. Waddington mode. I'll act my way through it, dish out a few detentions and achievement points here and there. I'll do it for my frère.

FRIDAY 5 APRIL

We did it, Sam. Everyone had a blast celebrating your life yesterday. Well, *blast* might be a stretch, but I'm too tired to find a better word. I'm zzzonked out in bed as I type this. And you – you're a box of ashes now, resting in a room called the Chapel of Rest.

The funeral party was bittersweet, let's say. Lots of laughing and crying, and even some dancing to 'Give it Up' by KC and The Sunshine Band, your grand finale. Vicky, sporting a luminous yellow dress, urged us on. When the song kicked in and your photo montage lit up the big screen, she hopped off the podium and gave her hips a good shake, practically edging us out of our seats. After a moment of hesitation, everyone joined in for a little boogie. It was the weirdest spectacle, Sam – like forcing a bunch of upset kids in detention to dance.

Should we have been dancing at a funeral? Weren't we supposed to be sad and serious? Tricky questions. But this was a funeral *party*, and you loved to dance, so it felt right to get up and *give it up*. That's why I ended on that song – it was that or 'Sexbomb,' courtesy of Welsh hunk Tom Jones, which would've been absolutely hilarious, but party-pooper Mum talked me out of it. Probably for the best. Can you imagine being laid to rest to 'Sexbomb'?

Getting everyone up and smiling, doing what you loved, it couldn't have gone any better. And we definitely needed a pick-me-up after 'The Power of Love' by Frankie Goes to Hollywood and 'My Heart Will Go On' by Celine Dion – yes, I threw in some tearjerkers because I know how much of a soppy soul you were.

I'll be honest, Samwells, I got awkward, dancing with my abysmal moves on show. I imagined you cackling in your coffin. You knew how much I hated dancing in front of people – stiff as a board, forgetting how to clap in time to a simple beat. Meanwhile, Mama J was giving it her all next to me, like a gospel singer, moving with pride and purpose. She was the first one up after Vicky's little shimmy. I followed Mum's lead, pretending it was just us two – the bros. In the end, I could only laugh at the situation. Realising I'd dug myself a hole by choosing to close on a dancy number and feeling like you'd finally got your payback for me breaking your femur.

***

Barely get a moment to write to you these days. I'm exhausted from juggling everything – organising, emailing, making phone calls, grieving, crying until my head hurts, comforting others, letting them comfort me. It's relentless, but I guess it's part and parcel of this fragile period.

Sue's been staying with us. Swardy Wardy, as Dad calls her – I think we inherited our knack of nicknames from him. She drove us to and from the funeral party, which was one less thing to think about. She's so considerate. Always has been. Mum's truly blessed with so many close pals.

We've been reminiscing about you over cups of tea, laughing at all your shenanigans. Like the time you lobbed bottles of shampoo and shower gel out of the bathroom window. You must've been about fifteen. Sue and Mum were sitting outside, blissfully unaware, as plastic bottles landed by their feet like they'd stumbled into a battlefield. I still wonder what ticked you off so much you felt the need to empty the bathroom out of the window. I bet it was something I said. Or Mum. Or Dad. Or maybe even Sue. Who knows? Poor Sue and Mum – wrong place at the wrong time. To be fair, I don't think you realised they were outside. Hope you didn't!

I miss your outbursts, brother. Your fire and passion. Though I definitely don't miss being on the receiving end. I didn't enjoy being on the battlefield with you, back when your arms were stronger, and you could cause some serious damage. I felt like Neo from *The Matrix* in your late teenage years, dodging cutlery, stationery, and whatever else you managed to get your hands on.

I'll never forget the time you nearly blinded me with a knife at the dinner table. You narrowly missed my left eye. You had some aim, Sam – hurling objects with speed and accuracy. You could've been a great darts player.

But look, I know now the outbursts weren't just you being a menace. So much of it was frustration – building up when your body wouldn't do what you wanted it to do. And there was all the medication that minced your mood. Anyone stuck in a chair like that would get fucked off easily. Still... maybe breaking your legs was my payback for all the times you launched shit at me.

We'll talk more about those outbursts another time. When I have more energy, more caffeine in my veins. In the meantime, let's blame it on the boogieman Douchebag Duchenne – the real villain of this story. I should head off now. Need to get ready; I'm going back to Chesil House with Dad. Never bloody stops. I'll make up some time later to talk.

Speak soon, Sam… 'The Hurler' Waddington.

***

Collecting your bits and bobs now from the memory table I set up at Chesil House. I took a slice of your bedroom and laid it out on a table – like you a Tracey Emin installation. Your Stoke City scarf, your mini flags from all the countries you visited, the event programmes from football matches and concerts, your *Titanic* ship, your nodding Mr. Bean toy. All that tacky trash you loved.

I'm also grabbing your photo collage – can't forget that. The Parents plan to hang it where I suggested: right across from the dining room table, so they can eat with their Sammy. Sammys, I should say – there's about fifty of your little round faces collaged together. Feels like I've already told you this.

Dad's nipped out to pay for the parking. We found a spot near King Alfred's statue. Good old King Alfred, bravely facing the Vikings, sword raised high, standing tall on a stone plinth almost as large as the statue itself. It's a powerful monument – and home to some powerful moments. You know this is where I first met Agathe. On our Tinder date, back in 2018 – when I had a fuller head of hair and a touch more allure. I thought it'd be a solid meeting spot. An iconic backdrop.

Here's a little behind-the-scenes for you, Sam. Before we met, I panicked and bought a packet of condoms from Tesco. It'd been a while since I'd been on a date, and I was woefully unprepared. Standing by the bus stop at King Alfred's, I practised my lines, smoothed my eyebrows, while the Durex pack bulged from my Levi's jacket. What a clown. Why did I wait until the last minute to buy condoms? What if my date spotted the box when I took off my jacket in the pub? She'd think I was a freak.

I even considered walking back to the train station and giving up on dating altogether, but then I saw this petite girl with red lipstick – though she now insists it was pink nude, Merh by MAC, if you were interested, Samuela – strutting towards me. Very cute, very sexy, I thought. I smiled and waved, but it came off more like a salute. Her lipstick smiled back at me.

'Hey. Agathe, right? Sorry if I pronounced it wrong.'

She snickered. 'No, that's fine! Hey.' Her voice was high-pitched, with an accent that sounded American, not French, like her profile stated.

We exchanged a polite hug. I tried not to lean in too close, praying she wouldn't feel my boxy bulge.

'You know, you look shorter than you do in your photos.'

Shut up, Jack. What are you even saying?

She laughed. I grinned like a clueless idiot. 'Oh really?'

'Yeah...I mean, it's a good thing.'

Just end me now.

For some reason, I decided to hug her again, completely forgetting about the bulge. 'It's great to finally meet you.'

'It's good to meet you too.' She glanced to the side, like she didn't know what to say, a little embarrassed. 'To The Black Boy then?'

'Let's do it!'

Calm down, Jack.

And off we went to The Black Boy – not sure that name would pass for a pub these days, Sam, but heigh-ho. I sipped cider while she opted for a vodka cranberry. We spoke about our lives, interests, exes, and the usual first-date gibberish. She aspired to be a fashion buyer; I fancied myself an artist. A perfect little disaster. Another round was ordered. She didn't notice the box of rubbers tucked away in my pocket. Success! We even shared a sneaky kiss outside, thanks to my winning line: 'Your lips look really kissable.' And just like that, bam. Instant connection. She must have a thing for weirdos.

And that's all you need to know about that evening, you cheeky bugger. Let's just say, we hit it off. The next morning, I was having my petit déjeuner with her, and two months later I was packing my suitcase for Lisbon. After picking up her Fashion Business and Marketing degree from the University of Winchester, she landed a six-month internship at a trendy concept store owned by one of her brother's friends. When she asked if I wanted to join her in the Portuguese capital, I didn't think twice. Bold move from your brosephine, but it felt right. I needed a bit of sun, a bit of me-time. I was at a crossroads after wrapping up my year at Pret a Manger in Winchester, trying to save for God knows what. An art studio in London? My future was foggy, but one thing was clear: Agathe was going to be part of it. I just knew.

Ouch, that sounded fromagey.

Dad's coming back now. We'll talk more about The Agatron later – I miss calling Agathe *The Agatron* around you; it never failed to crack you up.

***

Pulling into Granny's driveway to say hello. She loves you so much, Sam. Her special little grandchild. I've never seen her cry as much as she did yesterday, at your funeral party. Sitting behind her son, daughter-in-law, and last grandchild left to carry on the family name – moi – who were also crying their eyes out. Knowing that her other grandson – toi – was silently lying in a coffin in front of them, like her husband did a year before. It was too much for her. She left straight after the ceremony.

She talks to you and Grandad every day. There's a photo of you two on her bedside table. She showed me. She sleeps in a little single bed now. Listens to Classic Fm with a novel in her hands before sleepytime. So sweet. She's the best granny ever.

You meant the world to people. Big, old presence you were, like Grandad with his strong Yorkshire accent. *See this finger, see this thumb, in a minute you'll get some.* The one we'd spend hours impersonating. *Ello, Sam. Ow's it going, love? D'you want some carrits? Some tayters?* Everyone's saying how you're with him up there in the sky, giggling, being tickled by his granite hands, discussing watches. He loved buying you a wristwatch, didn't he? Seko was his fav.

CARRY ON

SATURDAY 6 APRIL

Sneaky message from 12 Sidders, Sam – Agathe's taking a long shower, so I've got a couple of minutes to spare.

We went to Marwell Zoo today with The Parents. I've got an annual membership there now, like Mum and Dad. It was only thirty-odd pounds for unlimited access to one of the best zoos in the country. Bargain, if you ask me. I love it there. You loved it there. And it's only a short drive from 12 Sidders.

Crazy how much space there is at Marwell: one hundred and forty acres of farmland. Our very own Hampshire Savannah. And what about that cracking gift shop, with all those cuddlies and clothing and random merch catering to all ages – your dream. Can't forget the beautiful array of animals on display too – Sandra the Sloth, Mohammed the Meerkat and Krupa the Kangaroo.

Ok, those are porkies – I got carried away. They don't have names. Maybe they do, actually, but I don't know them. We loved making up names for people, animals, anything that moved – or things that didn't; hello, Timothy Toothbrush and Jimmy Night-Splints. We'd kill time with ease, wouldn't we? Playing our dumb games and laughing until it hurt.

Yes! Gwarn, Sakaaa! Bukayo's scored a pen for The Arsenal! One-nil up against Brighton away from home. We need a win to go back to the top of the prem. Then, to maintain our position at the top, we need Liverpool to flop at The Kop – I'm watching footy as I write to you, Sam.

We wanted the Gooners to win the league so badly, didn't we? After narrowly missing out last season. They were our Premier League team. Stoke were our Championship team.

And Beastly Eastleigh FC our National League team. Greedy football fans! I'd cut off an arm to be watching this game with you. The run-in. Crunch time, where every game counts. Maybe you're watching the game in heaven. Do they have Sky up there? Sky Sports in the sky.

Sorry, that was poor.

***

Granny said I should be a writer – all because of the bang tidy *you*logy I wrote. She didn't say it like that – *bang tidy* – but you know what I mean. Everyone liked the *you*logy. People said it painted an honest picture of you, and it revealed a lot about you to those who didn't know you as well. All your little quirks and triumphs throughout your life. I was showing you off big time, Sambobs. Jack the Apostle.

Right, time to skedaddle and watch the rest of the game. Let's cross our fingers for the Goooners!

SUNDAY 7 APRIL

Hi Sambeleenoes.

I kept thinking about you while watching the football today. It's been a right old footy fest this weekend – Brighton v Arsenal, Man U v Liverpool, and now Tottenham v Notts Forest. Dad's here with me for this one, parked in his red leather chair with the footrest. I'm on the beige sofa, and you're somewhere in between in your wheelchair. That was our set up. The Waddington boys. Three in a row, watching the footy. Our one true love. The gift that keeps on giving, every weekend, without fail.

It's one of the few pastimes that keeps me going. Lately, all I want to do is watch football. Football, football, football. It always reminds me of you. Staring at twenty–two grown men jogging around on that luminous green pitch. Yes, please. We loved it. A feast for our eyes. And that sounded unintentionally homoerotic.

Anyway. I'm cooking dinner for The Parents tonight. Nothing too ambitious: quiche, ham, cheese, and a side salad. Nibbles. I had a big Sunday roast in Winchester with Agathe before she took the train back to London.

I'm going to miss her, Brother Gammon. Not as much as I miss you, but still. It scares me to go back to London. Back to Billy Bobs. I won't be near my Sammybobs. Your bedroombobs, your wheelchairbobs, your souvenirbobs, your smellbobs. I'll be far away in a small flat you never set foot – wheel – in.

People say you'll be there in spirit, with me in the big bad city. I guess I could believe that, since I'm already talking to you like you're still here, alive and kicking.

You know, I don't know how long I'll keep writing to you like this. I mean, I talk to you out loud and say *Sammyboys* a hundred times a day just to reassure myself you're still here, not forgotten. But writing to you while sitting or lying down feels different. Like you're a pen pal I'll never meet. I'm not entirely sure what my goal is with this ritual. Maybe I don't need one. You don't always need to know your destination, right?

Maybe I'm just on a treadmill with you. Going nowhere in particular. A treadmill to nowhere. Maybe we're just working things out. Or working out. We never went to the gym together, did we? I'm doing fifty press-ups a day, by the way. Gonna get me some muscles and sweat out my sadness.

I need to go for a sprinkle. Then I'll start making dinner.

***

It's been five weeks since you left us. Five weeks since our last conversation. I don't want to drift any further from the time you were breathing. These shark-infested waters are scary. They say time heals, but this healing feels a lot like forgetting. And I'm not ready to forget you. I'm not ready to let you go. I miss you, brother o'mine.

This lazy bitch of a brother still hasn't started dinner. But nobody's said a word because none of us really has an appetite. Grief will do that to you. I've been lying in bed doing zilch – well, not entirely true. I've been listening to Mum talk to Linda on the phone, slipping into her Trinidadian accent like she always does for her Sunday afternoon ritual. I know I'm eavesdropping, but the walls are thin and she's practically shouting half the time. She loves chatting with

Linda, dusting off that old Trinny twang from her girlhood days with her best buddy in the Caribbean.

She likes to reminisce about the days before children and Duchenne and a husband who stays up late watching horror movies – sorry, Dad. Before she lived in a house with three football-obsessed boys– we'll say Dad's an overgrown boy, and I doubt he'd argue with that. Sorry again, Dad.

Imagine growing up in the Caribbean, though. I'm kinda jealous of Mum's childhood. Surrounded by sunshine and sand and soca. Now that I'm older, I wish I could go back. Appreciate it properly. You could walk when we went to Trinidad and Barbados. 2003, I think. I don't remember much from that trip, just random fragments. Finding a cockroach in a bedroom. Buying a bracelet from a Rasta mon on the beach. Visiting an old man Mum knew as a child. I can't recall his name or even which island he lived on, but he gave us cartons of sweet fruit juice and claimed he had a croc in a nearby pond. Maybe he was fibbing, but I loved believing it. What a fun pet to have in the neighbourhood. I'm glad for Mum. It pleases me to hear her sweetening herself, laughing with her oldest friend, sharing memories. Just an hour before she was crying in front of the TV. It's hard seeing her like that, Sam, but I know she has to let it out.

I'm working up a sweat now, and a headache's brewing in this hot, compact room that used to be yours. I'll open the window. And then, I swear, I'm actually going to make that smorgasbord!

MONDAY 8 APRIL (MORNING)

Saw my first firecrest today – in Beastly Eastleigh of all places. Here's what went down.

I was walking along the River Itchen towards Shawford, dodging puddles on the path, taking in the nature, and winking at the animals, feeling like Snow-bloody-White. As well as the firecrest, I spotted a blackcap, a chiffchaff, a flurry of long-tailed tits, a greenfinch, a nuthatch, and a little egret, along with the usual suspects: robins, great tits, blue tits, wrens, sparrows, blackbirds, wood pigeons, and mallards. A couple of roe deer even showed up. Beautiful.

I had my bird identifier app, Merlin, ready to help me out. I like using it when I'm out in the open, just in case I come across any hidden treats. It's like Shazam for birders. I quietly held my phone up to record the sounds and waited patiently. About twenty minutes into my walk, Merlin alerted me of a nearby firecrest. When I saw its picture on my screen, I was gobsmacked. I'd almost given up on locating those sneaky birds years ago. At first, I thought it might be a mistake, but Merlin's reliable, so it had to be right.

'Where are you, you little fireball?' I whispered.

I knew these chirpy chappies liked large, evergreen trees. I spotted a tall fir tree beside me.

'Bullseye.' My voice still a hush.

Switching from Merlin to YouTube, I typed in *firecrest call*, played the first video, turned up the volume, and pointed my phone at the tree, hoping to attract the bird. It didn't take long. Mr. Firecrest came right over, thinking I was one of its own. But it couldn't find the other 'bird', even though it heard the call. After I noticed its bright red streak on its head and watched it hop from branch to branch, I turned off the YouTube clip and continued my walk along the River Itchen. Mission accomplished.

I felt a bit cruel teasing the bird with my phone, making it think it had a friend nearby when it was just a screen. That's what these love letters are too, aren't they? Just me calling out through a screen, wishing you could swoop in like Mr. Firecrest.

***

This morning was a busy one, Sam. We returned your laptop and other equipment to SPECTRUM. Good old SPECTRUM. You'll be sorely missed there. You were the best hate-crime coordinator in town. We saw your bossman, Ian – the first guest (after me, The Agatron, The Parents, and Swardy Wardy) to arrive at your funeral party, and the last to leave. What a brilliant boss he must've been, promptly offering you full-time employment after your volunteering stint at SPECTRUM post-uni. I'm glad you had supportive people like him in your professional life. People who were also dependent on a wheelchair. People who understood you and your limitations without explanation.

We also met two of your other colleagues, whose names I can't recall, but they were lovely. They came to your funeral party too. My favourite part of visiting your workplace was seeing your desk in your office – where you spent two days a week, busying yourself away. It was like you'd never left. There was a pug mug, some stationery, and notepads with work-related scribbles. You took your job so seriously, and that made your big brother smile.

On our way back to 12 Sidders, we stopped at the Henry Ford garage in Beastly Eastleigh to return the accessible van. Another tough trip. But I laughed after I said, 'See you,

Sam the Van,' as we left the Ford Independence. The van wasn't you; it was just a vessel that got you from a to b. But you spent countless hours strapped into the back, off on your many adventures. I'll always remember how much effort it took to get you in there – lowering the ramp, securing the hooks to the front and back of your chair, fastening the seatbelt around both you and your chair like you were Harry Houdini. There was no escaping. Without that van, traveling around the country would've been tricky, and we certainly did a lot of it. So many family holidays in the Sam Van. Let's reminisce about a few of them soon, ok?

I'll feel the void for your trusty wheels, Sam.

***

I'm in your room taking photos of your chair. We're planning to sell it – try to, at least. I'm capturing shots from the side, front, and backside. I could make a video, but I want to avoid highlighting the tears in the fabric. I'm sure we can sell it, despite its lived-in aesthetic. The upholstery can be easily replaced, and the chair's still in pretty good condition, considering it's five years old. You've warmed the seat for the next bum-bound.

I'd do anything to have you back in your chair, so I wouldn't have to sell it.

I'm trying to be happy, forcing myself to most of the time, but I'm lost without you. I feel as empty and cold as your sleeping quarters. Nothing seems to fill this emptiness or warm me up.

***

I strongly dislike the school I'm at, Sam – sorry, lots of offloading today, and not just the literal kind we've been doing with your van, laptop, and chunky chair.

I've not liked many schools, to be honest. Maybe I just have a general dislike of school. I didn't enjoy it as a student either. I had some close friends at Kings', but it was still torture. Taking the yellow bus, getting bullied, getting pummeled – it took its toll. I never wanted to return to a school after leaving Kings'. And now, here I am, spending my weekdays in an environment I couldn't bear as a kid. How bizarre is that? Life really is like a box of choclits.

I never imagined I'd become a professeur. I was always so shy and insecure. Speaking in front of a group gave me boiling-hot ears and panic attacks. But talking to teenagers is different; they rarely listen to you. With adults – or people my own age – I still get nervous. Don't know why. Maybe it's imposter syndrome. Or fear of judgement. I'm trying to overcome this stage fright, but I'm not sure I ever will.

I was in a staff meeting the other day – before you died, that is – with teachers from other departments and I was dreading the thought of speaking in front of them. So much so, I asked the teacher leading the session not to call on me because I have anxiety and struggle with public speaking. Mad, innit?

I always envied how you could just get up on stage to perform, sing, dance, or speak to a large audience at work. You fed off the crowd.

Really going off on one here, Sam. Just making up for all the calls we haven't had.

I loved our talks about anything and everything – birds, football matches, funny things the kids said, your latest Amazon finds, girlfriend problems. Your support meant a lot, especially when I felt misunderstood. You were the best at listening, always lifting my spirits.

MONDAY 8 APRIL (EVENING)

Hi Sam.

It's half-nine. The moon's out, as well as my phone. I'm going to leave you a handful of voice recordings while I walk around Beastly Eastleigh. Once I'm back in my bedroom, I'll type it up on my laptop. I'll need to keep the volume low while I listen; don't want Mum and Dad thinking I'm talking to myself. Thin walls, remember. Hopefully, they'll be watching TV or on their phones – Mum with her ASMR videos in bed and Dad with *The Thing* or *The Poltergeist* on downstairs. I know this sounds odd, me typing up my voice note to you, but I'm a grieving mess right now, so let your brother be, ok?

I plan to turn these conversations into a book. That's the plan now. *I'm on a Journey to See You, Sam*. It's happening. You'd be happy to hear that. You always wanted people to pursue their passions and creating is mine. I need to hunch over and make things – whether it's pretty little pictures or pretty little sentences. It's a detox for my soul. Helps me cope with the blues.

I think I stepped on a snail – heard the shell crack. Whoopsy daisy. Hard to see those little guys. You don't normally look at your feet – especially at night – when you walk. Well, you definitely didn't; you were focused on your wheels.

***

Sky's a deep blue, the clouds tinged with purple. A handful of stars are peeking through the gaps in the clouds. My good old buddy Hugh mentioned something about stars the other day. He said that when he lost someone dear, he imagined them as a star in the sky, and he plans to think of you as one of those stars, shining the brightest, the next time he looks up. I like that idea, corny as it sounds; you as a blazing spheroid, over a billion years old. Indestructible. Mostly.

He's been a rock-solid friend. At your funeral party, he plated up lunch for me and insisted I sit and eat and take a break from playing host. He was right; I was shattered and needed to eat. I was speaking to everyone, pretending I was a maître d' rather than a grieving brother. My primary school buddy's a keeper. He mentioned running the marathon for you next year. He wants to raise money for a charity. What a Hughmungous gesture. What a lad.

To my right is the road that leads to the new cemetery. Just by the ancient Stoke Park Woods. Mum's thinking about putting your ashes there. Did you ever visit it? I haven't. I'll have to check it out soon. Give it my seal of approval. I want your ashes nearby, somewhere I could visit easily. I could take a train from London, stay at 12 Sidders, walk to the cemetery, see your plaque, and—

Fuck. It's hard thinking about things like that, Sam, let alone saying it out loud. It's weird. Feels like I'm actually speaking to you through this recording.

I know you can tell I'm crying right now. I don't want you to feel bad when I cry, or when Mum, Dad, Granny and Megan are hurting too. It's just your passing is too much to bear at times. I've lost a massive part of my identity. All the good moments, the joy you brought into my life – it's all vanished. Now I'm left wondering who the hell I am. I know it's not your fault; it's just some cruel twist of fate. It could've been me in that wheelchair.

You never wanted to be seen as 'Sam who struggles with Duchenne.' You refused to let that define you. You were Sam.

Sam the Sam. Yes, you were disabled. It was hard to ignore you in that chair. But you made sure to stand up to that deadly disease like a bully in a school playground. You stole its lunch money, gave it peanuts and wedgies, and told it to stay away. I know you did. Dooshyboy hated living with you.

The tears have stopped. For now, at least.

***

Random, but don't you think it's weird how we're Stoke City fans, and *Stoke* keeps popping up in every corner of Hampshire? Bishopstoke, Stoke Heights, Stoke Park Woods, Stoke Park Surgery, Stoke Common Road. Coincidence, much? Or maybe it's a sign we should hold Stoke City as close to our hearts as Dad does? City 'til we die. Well, that box you've already ticked off. Sorry.

The club's part of us, Samwells, even if they're having a tough old time finding their identity of late. Still a fun team to support. Great logo, with the kilns nodding to their pottery roots. Great kit: red and white stripes. Great mascot: Pottermous. Great nickname: The Potters. Great managers: Tony Waddington – sadly no relation – Tony Pulis, and your favourite, Marky Sparky Hughes, who pulled off three straight ninth-place finishes in the Prem. Not an easy feat. It's all gone a bit downhill since then.

But now we've got The Arsenal! Quite the step up from Stoke, hey? I hope they win the title. We spoke about them a lot this season and last. They gave us something to look forward to – some regular, good-quality football for once. Supporting Stoke so religiously while watching their decline didn't do our mental health any favours. Thanks, Dad, for being a midlander and making us support a team like Stoke Shitty. At least The Arsenal take the edge off. Tactical, hey.

The Gooners are playing Bayern Munich tomorrow. Champions League quarter-final – I know, right! I'll try to live-stream it. Just imagine beating Bayern and making it to the semis – one game from silverware. You'd be over the moon. You'd scribble the fixture down in your 2024 diary.

**CHAMPIONS LEAGUE SEMI-FINAL 1ST LEG –
EMIRATES STADIUM – 8PM**

***

It's getting late now, Sam. You'd probably be in bed, fresh from your shower, tuning into *Match of the Day* – no, that's a lie. You'd be on the phone to Megan, gearing up for an hour phone call, full of 'I love you's' and 'I miss you's.' She's in··· where is it? Louisiana? The Deep South. I'm glad she's there, enjoying the country music, seeing the sights, reminiscing about the short but thrilling ride she had with you. I bet she writes to you every day. Or sends you voice recordings. I'm so happy you found her. And I'm so happy she found you. You did what partners in crime do: you helped each other out.

Agathe's been a big help to me. And I support her too – maybe not as much as she supports me. I'll see her on Wednesday. I'm heading back to London, my *home* home. Haven't been back since you passed. I'll be thinking about you constantly, Sam – when I'm cooking and shitting and whatnot. Sorry, but it's true: I often think of you when I poo.

I'm laughing and crying like I did when I was five – ADHD kid through and through. How no-one clocked it is beyond me. Different times in the nineties, I guess. And maybe there was more of a focus on you and your legs, than me and my restlessness.

I'm sorry; I know you'd hate to see me hurting. Please don't feel like you caused this.

You're twenty-seven now, a grown man. That's how I'll remember you – a strong man in his prime. Not as a wrinkly, old man like I'll become, unless something unexpected happens – like getting hit by a car tomorrow. I'll have to live many more years without you, more than the years we shared. People say it gets easier, that the grief stays the same size. That it doesn't disappear. That your experiences help you grow with time, and you start to see grief as less of a disabling force. Time, those experiences, and your growth are the three vital ingredients to help you digest the grief. I've witnessed it. Mum losing Grandma, Dad losing Grandad. At first, the grief consumed them, but they soon grew around it. They became bigger than their grief. It can happen for me too.

***

I'm walking past the defibrillator on the community centre wall. It glows orange in the dark, like a big, shiny sweet. I think they've given me PTSD. Dad used this exact one when the kind neighbour rushed it over – trying to save you. He should never have had to do that.

I picture Dad as a curly-haired boy in Staffordshire, in a little house in Eccleshall, with a younger Granny and Grandad and two sisters all orbiting him, keeping him safe. Did he ever imagine he'd have a disabled son who'd die just nine days before turning twenty-seven? I doubt it.

I wish I'd been there at 12 Sidders to take on that burden. I would've given you chest compressions, opened your airways, blown air into your lungs, called the emergency services – juggling everything like some Hindu god with too many arms. I would've been the one watching you shutdown beneath me.

I keep telling Dad not to blame himself. If the paramedics couldn't save you with all their tools, then he didn't stand a chance. It wasn't his fault. Nor was it Mum's. Just your time, wasn't it? Our gift had to be returned. I think I just stepped on another snail. His time too. Not sure why I gave the snail a sex – I don't know my male and female snails.

Every time I see that defibrillator, my stomach sinks a little, and I remember that large round mark the machine embossed on your chest. I ran my fingers over it. Cold – like Iron Man's arc reactor.

Now I'm picturing you as a superhero. A smile's forming on my sticky face.

I'm at the front door now, Sam. A steaming-hot shower awaits. Then I'll type up this bad boy. Might even treat myself to a couple of *Avatar: The Last Airbender* episodes. Yes, I'm thirty, and yes, I still watch cartoons, and yes, that's ok – so leave it, brother.

Ok. Speak soon, Sam.

TUESDAY 9 APRIL

I've been writing to you for six days straight. How about that? Good form. Consistent. And this six-day streak hasn't been deliberate. Oh no. It hasn't been forced. Just felt right. I've got some more time on my hands before heading back to Londres et ma petite amie.

I'm in Mum's art room, surrounded by drawers overflowing with textured paper and paints, and colourful gel prints of leaves and flowers tacked to the walls. The two portable radiators next to me are on full blast, keeping me toasty. It was never accessible for you because of the steps, but goodness gracious me, it gets chilly in here. Amazing how our mama's got her own art studio now, using it? I can't even picture the old garage before it split in two – Mum's art cave and Dad's mini garage.

I have my weekly counselling session with Fiona shortly. Naomi House and Jacksplace set me up with her after I rang their Family Support Helpline – just after your Christmas Eve leg break. I was in a state. I knew I needed help, and I knew the NHS waiting list would swallow me whole. Naomi House and Jacksplace supported families like ours – families of disabled children and young adults who stayed at the hospice – so I tried my luck. They understood right away and arranged a session with a counsellor like it was a matter of urgency.

I've had something ridiculous like twenty sessions now. We do this thing called talking therapy, not CBT, which I was happy about. I had CBT at uni. I didn't like being told how to think, what to change. I was and still am quite stubborn. But with Fiona, I can let off steam and speak my mind for an hour while she listens and prompts me with questions every now and then. She's wonderful. Everyone at Naomi House and

Jacksplace are. They're hands down the best charity I know. So selfless. I loved visiting you there when you were younger – Naomi House during your childhood and Jacksplace in your teens and early twenties. You'd stay for a week or so during holidays to give Mum and Dad some much-needed respite, and for you to be able to have some quality Sam time. You could do whatever you liked – board games, video games, swimming in the hydrotherapy pool, arts and crafts, trips to the cinema. They spoilt you rotten.

But I'm not in the mood for this session. I'm tired. I don't know if I have the energy to talk and be the centre of attention for an hour. I'd rather go get some lunch – I barely ate breakfast, just a small bowl of porridge. Can't survive without breaky, you know me. And Dad wants to take me to the New Forest later for some birdwatching. He's bringing his binoculars. He's well up for it, like he has been ever since I got into birdwatching. I agreed to go since the weather's nice, and I can't say no to birds. Maybe I'll spot a goshawk, but that's probably wishful thinking. They're secretive little bastards.

Counselling first. It's good for me. Talking things through, unravelling my thoughts. And I like Fiona. She used to be a teacher like me, but she didn't enjoy it. She prefers counselling, and she's good at it.

Strange to think we started talking before you died. She was so taken aback by your death, Sam – I feel like I'm saying *death* and *died* more often now, which is a positive sign, right? She couldn't hold back her tears. One week I was saying I missed you because you lived far away, and the next I was saying I missed you because you weren't alive anymore.

I didn't go into your bedroom this morning – practice for London, I guess.

WEDNESDAY 10 APRIL

I'm stuck in Westminster, waiting for the transfer to Ealing Common, where Agathe will meet me. The station is humming with bodies and noise, and anxiety is sitting heavy in my chest. It isn't the soon-to-be-wife I'm dreading – it's the thought of returning to my daily routine. Tomorrow means Billy Bobs, and I can't be bothered to go back. Putting on a smile, pretending everything's ok. Erghh. If anyone asks, *How are you?* or *How was your Easter holidays?* I swear I might just lose it and punch them on the nose.

Sorry – I'm also feeling quite angry. People annoy me. Those who stroll around, using their legs like it's no big deal, counting their steps on their silly little watches. Those who don't have to sleep with a ventilator every night. And don't get me started on the people who are older than you, who are still living. None of it's fair. You deserve to still be here.

Van Morrison's grumbling in my ears as I write this. He was a ball of rage. Still is. But he had a lot of love too – music, literature, spirituality, nature. A love for love. He loved to love, and I do too. That's why this whole mess is hitting me hard.

Speaking of love: ya gal Megan got a tattoo the other day. But you probably knew that already. I still like to think of you as an all-knowing, omnipresent deity, not just trapped with me and my misery; you're here, there, everywhere – keeping tabs on Megan, The Parents, Granny, and all your friends. Seeing what we're all up to. Making sure we're not changing the layout of your room too much. Keeping your souvenirs intact.

Megan's wrist tattoos are something else – she sent me a photo on Facebook. Colourful flowers, two Scrabble tiles leaning against each other – an *S* for Sam the Scrabble enthusiast and, yes, you guessed it, an *M* for Megan – not S&M in the other sense. Imagine that! I'd love to know what you think of it. Having your name permanently inked on someone else's skin. I wonder what that would feel like⋯ Agathe doesn't have my name scribbled on her. Yet.

And what about Mum's new tat? She only went and did it – an *S* Scrabble tile inked on her arm. Just like you were planning. Her first tattoo – what a brave mama we've got. A tiny, permanent square in honour of her son. Didn't Morrissey once sing something about scratching a name on an arm with a fountain pen – and how it means you really love that person?

I find it funny that you wanted the letter *S* tattooed on you. No deep meaning – just an *S* for Sam and your love of Scrabble. So random.

THURSDAY 11 APRIL

I've plunged into a shit pit, Brother Sam, like those teenage years I thought I'd left behind. I'm drowning in hopelessness and agitation, and I feel like any second now, a demon's going to appear from around the corner to gobble me up. Maybe it has already, and that's why it's so bloody dark. I've lost all motivation to do anything. No drive to enjoy myself. I'm just trudging through the dark days, like I'm stuck in Hieronymus Bosch's *Hell* – that medieval Dutch artist I used to be obsessed with, known for his surreal paintings crammed with naked people, demons, and other freaky creatures. Creepy stuff.

They say there are five phases of grief: depression, anger, denial, bargaining, and acceptance. Right now, depression is the loudest. Feels like it'll be with me forever, like the blood and guts inside me. Great. Can't bloody wait.

Heart, Brain, Bones – meet Depression. He's here for the long haul. Think of him as Blood's sad cousin. He won't be keeping me alive, just miserable. He'll be flowing his gloomy juices through my veins all day every day.

I'm taking my anti-depressants. Like you did when you were feeling low. Dealing with your condition and the limitations that came with it. You'd be proud – me tryna fix meself up. One little tablet a day. Fifty milligrams of Sertraline. I've been taking these pills since November, right after I was diagnosed with ADHD. Just a month or so before the jaccident with your left leg. Perfect timing.

I didn't want to fill myself with pills like a box of Tic-Tacs. I didn't want them to numb me or make me reliant. But I couldn't see any alternative. I've tried mindfulness, Vipassana meditation, exercising, eating the right foods, CBT, more Vipassana meditation, this time at a ten-day meditation retreat in Kiev. But the depression still squats in my body, putting a glum filter over everything. That's why I'm giving the meds a go. They say it takes about six months to feel the magic. I'm on month five now. In thirty days or so, I'll be feeling fit as a fiddle. Let's see. I'm hoping this, plus the talking therapy with Fiona, will sort me out. For the time being, anyway.

I'm worried this book will be an excuse for me to moan and groan about my life. And I do love a good moan. I'm the Howlin' Wolf of whining. It's tempting, you know.

Agathe told me to dig a little deeper with my writing. She's read some parts, along with a few other trusty people. She seems satisfied with how everything reads so far. She gave me her typical nod of approval, saying it has a nice flow and casual style. Communicates well. But she also feels a lot of it's just me saying how much I miss you. Can't say she's entirely wrong. She's always been frank and French with her feedback – no beating it around the bush.

She's got a point: me blabbering on about how much I miss you, like you were some sort of saint. Saint Sam. Sorely missed. It would be a dull read if all I did was moan and groan into the midnight and grieve and worship till the cows come home. I guess I need to sprinkle in some real-life insights. Life living as the sibling of a disabled brother. Potential readers might want to hear about that. Because, honestly, not many get it. They see it from the outside. The family with the disabled child. The struggle. Bless The Waddingtons. Yes – The Waddingtons struggle, more than they can imagine. I wish I could tell them just how bloody difficult it really is. I wish I could shout and scream it.

I think I need to open up a bit more. To you, to myself. I need to dig deeper into this struggle. What's it all about? The know-how's say to write about what you know. Well, this chaotic life is what I know. And it isn't an ordinary life. It has a USP – you. But hey, people also write about things they know diddly squat about – magical worlds in cupboards and wizarding schools in the countryside – so I'm really not sure anymore.

What do you think? Should I go for it? Let my guard down?

Go for it, Jack. Dig deep, brother. Like your deep, dark depression!

Very funny. But you're right – I will. Talking about my depression is digging a little deeper, I guess. I told you it wasn't your fault I'm super depressed. And that's true, to some extent.

I think my ADHD has a big part to play. Getting that diagnosis last year gave me some form of closure. Turns out, depression and anxiety are common side effects of ADHD. I always wondered where that little double act came from. Makes sense now. It doesn't make everything go away, though. It does quite the opposite. It's all coming to the surface now – all my messy parts I've been hiding over the years. They call it unmasking. I'm letting the weird, wacky Jacky out to play. The one who gets exhausted, overwhelmed, fidgety, restless, runs out of things to say, overshares, forgets things, obsesses over things, finds it hard to see things through, intensely focusses on one thing, feels everything at once, interrupts people, finishes their sentences, gets stage fright, has a million thoughts racing through their head but can't spit any of them out, finds eye contact like staring into the sun, has difficulties managing anger – and a lot of other hot, steamy shit.

Wow. Take a breath, Jackyboy.

In the second message I wrote to you on your death day, thirty-nine days ago, I promised to be honest with you. And that's what I'll do now: I'm about to tell you something I've never shared with you – or anyone, really. I've kept it buried, mostly from myself. Bottling it up like red red wine. But that's not healthy, right? Time to face the music, just like I've come to accept my neurodiverse mind.

One, two, three – I think most of my sadness comes from having you in my life. The disabled brother.

There, I said it. And now I'm grimacing like I've sunk my teeth into a lemon.

Having you as a brother was the best thing that's ever happened to me. I mean that. But it's also been one of the hardest things to deal with. And that's not to do with your character, your unique brand of Samness. It's fundamentally to do with the fact that you had a disability. A life-threatening illness. Even though I don't remember it, learning about your disability back when I was a child at Upham frightened me big time. The thought of growing up, getting older, facing the inevitable. I didn't want to go through with it. I didn't want to grow up, knowing you'd eventually stop being able to walk. I didn't want to know that you'd die young.

***

Nope. The D word's definitely still a trigger – I burst into tears writing it in the previous paragraph. I had to leave the room and get some fresh West London air.

I'm back now, digging deeper. It hurts like hell, the tears are rolling, but I'm doing it. Maybe letting it all out in the open will help me. Maybe it'll cure my depression.

Realising you'd stop walking and perish – we'll use *perish* instead of the D word, as if you're a rotten fish! – sometime during your twenties or thirties was difficult to accept as a child. I was a shy, nervy, twitchy kid as it was. Then having to deal with that bombshell about my younger brother's illness. It set me off. At least, I think that's what happened. I'm not too sure. My memory's rubbish. Thinking back to primary school's a big ask. It's a blurry period in my life. I guess I tried to block out the inevitable – you vanishing from my life. And I've been blocking it out ever since. I'm still blocking it out, in a way. I still can't believe you aren't here. That's why I'm writing to you.

It was hard talking to anyone about what would happen to you. I got stage fright and frogs in my throat. I didn't want to bring it up with Mum and Dad; I didn't want to remind them of their youngest son's fate. It was the elephant in the room for a long time. I couldn't even bring myself to speak to you about it. It was just this unspoken truth we both knew.

I can't imagine what it was like for you, knowing you'd live half the life of the average person. It must've been terrifying. For most, perishing is this vague concept that's far away in the future, when we're old and crooked. Sure, people worry about it, some turning to religion, leaning on faith to ease their fear of what's lurking on the other side, but you got handed a sentence when you were still a child. And you just had to deal with that.

Maybe I should've spoken to you about it. Would that have been a good idea? How the hell would I have started that conversation? We never spoke about perishing – your perishing, I mean. Not many brothers talk about their upcoming perishings. But it was on my mind. I was going to lose you at some point. I didn't know how I'd cope without you. I was shit-scared about what lay ahead. I just wanted to stay young and watch *Mr. Bean* with you. Maybe that's why I liked being Mr. Immature around you. Staying safe from the future.

***

I've stopped crying now, Sam. I stepped away from my laptop to wipe my tired face; the dried snot and tears started to itch. Now I feel a bit more refreshed. I also changed the album I was listening to – Sigur Ros's '( )' album playing in the background wasn't helping. It's a harrowing listen but also a gorgeous one. You know, Jónsi sings in a made-up language called Hopelandic on that album – like The Cocteau Twins, or scatt singing in jazz, the voice serving as another instrument. I love all that gobbledygook.

My pin board's thriving, by the way, and I'm not even sorry for it. Agathe got me this A2 cork board last year, and I've crammed over two hundred pins on it. There's just a sliver of empty space left, begging for four or five more pins to complete the masterpiece. Not sure what happens when it's full. Do I start a new one, or will I feel satisfied with the full board and quit while I'm ahead? Job well done, onto something new. Would save me some cash, right?

I splurged £18 on two Jane Austen pins at a gift shop near Winchester Cathedral the other day. She isn't even one of my favourite writers. Crazy. Oh well – had to do it for the cork board's sake. I'm a collector, just like you were. Money? Who gives! You saw a gap in your hodgepodge of oddities and made sure to fill it. Taxidermy rat playing a fiddle – *yes please.* Velvet top hat? – *sure, why not?* Old-fashioned leather football? – *get on my shelf, you beauty.*

I'm back at Billy Bobs now, Sam. Got home about an hour ago. First day was an INSET day – thankfully no teaching, just planning and meetings. I thought I'd be a bundle of nerves, but I managed to walk in without throwing any nose punches. Lots of chitchat and *How are you's?* but I survived like Gloria Gaynor. I even chimed in during the department discussions, getting my voice out there. Sharing my ideas on how to improve the department etc.

I've always been good at finding things to polish up like a shoe – perfectionist at heart. That's why I'm a good art teacher. Always telling my students to refine their work and look for the finer details. Make sure it's shipshape, seamless like a Vermeer. And if they say they're finished, I make them zoom in and find the mistakes – the bits that don't quite look right. They definitely think I'm weird, but I can live with that. All my art teachers were weird.

Alright, I gone now.

P.S. I meant what I said about you being the best thing that's ever happened to me.

GETAWAY

FRIDAY 12 APRIL

Holiday time, Samwells.

I'm on a busy train to Amersham, squished next to The Agatron, and we can hardly contain our excitement. We're fizzing, buzzing, positively quivering for our little weekend escape to the Cotswolds.

Why the sudden need for a holiday, you ask?

I'll tell you why, Sammyboys.

A couple of sessions back, Fiona asked what I wanted for myself, and it hit me: I'd been so busy playing cheerleader for everyone else since you left, I hadn't paused to wonder what muggins here actually needed. What did I want, besides having you back and watching *Mr. Bean* or a football match together?

At first, I hadn't the foggiest. But after a bit of head-scratching, I told Fiona I needed a leafy interlude – even if just for the weekend. A quiet nook in England's pleasant pastures where I could kick back and read and stop feeling like a sad Jacky-sack.

And now here I am – leaning my head against the cool window, watching the scenery smudge past me, like I'm the main character in a daft but enchanting coming-of-age film.

SATURDAY 13 APRIL

Future wife and husband went on a long walk today, along what they call the five villages route. As the name suggests, you encounter five charming villages along the fourteen-kilometre trek. You would've adored it, codger.

Actually, that's not true at all. You wouldn't have been able to access most of the walk, apart from the occasional pavements through the villages, and even if you could brave the fields and lakeside paths, the luscious greenery wouldn't have exactly tickled your pickle.

I keep saying this to Dad since you left: that nature wasn't your thing. That you thrived in the hustle and bustle of towns, shops, restaurants, and those delightful little gift shops. Accessible places. I guess I wasn't off the mark? Maybe you associated nature with inaccessibility and coldness. You'd get nippy in your chair if you stayed outside too long, even if you were bundled up like a burrito – wrapped up in your hats, gloves, scarves, and electric blankets. Sitting still all the time didn't help – no footsteps to warm you up, less muscle tissue to keep the heat in. You felt the cold more than most.

Why do I keep making this point to Dad? That the outdoors wasn't exactly your cup of herbal tea. I think it's because I'm trying to connect to him, especially now that you're gone. I've felt a twinge of envy towards your bond with him. You two were inseparable, always in sync. He was your main carer, your main man. You were his everything. That's how I saw it, anyway.

Maybe I feel this urge to connect with our papa J now that he's on his own, without his Samson. I want to remind him of what we share – our love of nature, for instance.

We can bond over this. We can enjoy it together. Samwells didn't care for it the way we do – our love of scenery and wild animals and birds and rivers. The great outdoors. Enjoy these things. Sam would've wanted that. He wanted everyone in his circle to be happy. He'd want you to appreciate nature's beauty and find some peace in it. I'm here to help you do that. I know you haven't got many friends – you've always been a family man. And even though your family's getting smaller these days, you're not in this alone. I'm here. We'll climb the Ben this Summer together!

Sam was amazing. A real gem. But he wasn't perfect – he wasn't a nature-boy. We are. And maybe that's our ticket to surviving this torrid time: nature. It doesn't sugarcoat. Things die, bodies rot, things bloom again. Grief's just another season. It'll turn. We won't feel sad like this forever.

SUNDAY 14 APRIL

Morning, Samwells.

I can hear robins, blackbirds, and wrens chirping outside our cosy little Airbnb here in Amersham. There are probably a few more feathered friends lurking around – like a sparrowhawk, patiently waiting for its next meal. Just like me – I'm bloody starving. Me and my rapid metabolism. The Agatron's asleep. In about an hour, we'll be heading to Marlow, a fancy little town on The Thames, for our breakfast at the Michelin-starred restaurant. Living it large, brother.

I can sense your envy. I know how much you liked to wine and dine. You groovy gastronome.

Unfortunately, this place isn't accessible – as I discovered from a photo online that showed a big step and a narrow doorway.

You've always had to make do with whatever was accessible to you. Lots of things you had to miss out on, yet you never complained. You accepted your limitations and looked for alternatives, without wasting a second. Time was sacred for you.

Imagine if everything was disabled-friendly – ramps all around, no steps, no steep curbs, doors wide enough for a parade. It would be even better if disabilities didn't exist at all, but I guess the universe has a twisted sense of humour.

People keep telling me to chill out and switch off this weekend – just what a pinball-machine of a mind like mine likes to hear. To stop overthinking. To stop thinking about you. But they have no idea I'm scribbling to you, furiously, every moment I get. It's a bad habit I can't shake.

Mum mentioned she dreamt you were standing, not trapped in that wheelchair of yours. Not back when you wore your KAFOS, or when you were little with your beefy calves and tiptoe feet – classic signs of Duchenne – but as an adult. I struggled to picture that. I don't have images of a foot-to-ground you, only a bottom-to-chair you. That's the you I'm familiar with.

But I have been dreaming about you. Quite often. And let me tell you, some of those dreams are pretty bonkers.

Once, I had this wild dream where you were flying through the clouds in your chair, like it had a jet pack or something. You were out on a shopping spree, floating through aisles in the sky, packed with sour sweets, souvenirs, and wheelchair accessories – headrests and footplates, that sort of thing. You had a shopping list in one hand, which you peeked at now and then. You looked dead serious, like you were about to make the biggest purchase of your life.

I like dreaming of an airborne you.

Did you ever envision yourself standing? Like Mum did in her dream? Not in a chair. A future you. Or a past you. Any you, really. How did you see yourself in Beddybyeland? Did your chair ever feature in your dreams? Or did you walk? Did your dreams reflect a subconscious wish to be free of Duchenne?

Why didn't I ever hoist you onto the psychoanalytic couch and grill you with these pressing questions when you were still around?

Too late now.

Gotta bounce, Sam. The queen's awoken. Bonjour, ma chérie. She's caught me typing away on my Word app. She's about to get funny that I'm writing to you. And so she should

– it's meant to be our weekend away together. Off with my head!

Speak soon.

***

Guess what we had for breakfast? Only Staffordshire oatcakes! Not often you see those glorious pancakes served in fancy restaurants. The chef at The Coach fried them with cheese and thick, juicy bacon, and they tasted delicious. I still prefer them sweet, soaked in butter and honey. My childhood treat.

Remember our trips to Stoke-on-Trent to cheer on the Mighty Potters at the Brit? Dad would swing by that big Asda and fill the car with three million packs of Staffy oatcakes. Back at 12 Sidders, they'd go straight in the freezer, rationed out for our enjoyment till our next pilgrimage to The Potteries, which was usually a year later. We went once a year, Sam! Dedicated Hampshire Stokies, weren't we? Ta, Dad.

And guess what else? The restaurant turned out to be accessible, after all. Google lied to me; they must've added a ramp recently. A large American man came in, looking for a table for himself and his larger wife, who rolled in on wheels. The waiter regretfully informed the couple that there were no tables that could accommodate a wheelchair.

'I'm sorry,' he said, genuine concern written on his freshly shaven face.

The American scanned the small restaurant and huffed. 'Well, not to worry. We'll try another time.'

The only free spot was a small table next to me and Agathe, but there wasn't enough space for a wheelchair.

Then something magical happened. Agathe placed her coffee down, cleared her throat, and said, 'Hey – sorry, excuse me. We can move to the smaller table, and you can have ours, if you like? There's more space, for the wheelchair.'

I glanced at my fiancé and felt a tingle down my spine. I was about to suggest it too, but The Frenchy beat me to it. She's a thoughtful little mademoiselle, isn't she?

It's five in the afternoon and I'm on the train back to London, feeling like a deflated balloon. I mean, I knew I always would. This weekend away in the Chilterns with Agadoodoos was never going to fix my gloom; it was just a temporary escape for my worn-out brain.

My world was better with you in it, even if you lived a good seventy miles away in Beastly. Now that you're not here, my world is worse. Simple as that. Yes, things are becoming deceptively brighter, with spring trying to cheer things up and summer around the corner, but I just can't be bothered with it all. I'd trade all the blooming flowers for a night at 12 Sidders, helping you get ready for your evening shower.

The Parents would be in the living room, glued to some corny reality show that Mum roped Dad into, and we'd be upstairs in your room, all stations go. Your carer would be on their day-off, so I'd be subbed in for the evening, giving Mum and Dad a wee break.

'Hello, Mister Sam. How may I be of assistance this evening?'

'You know the drill, Brother Jack.'

'You're right. That I do. That I do.'

First, I'd lift you from your chair to your bed, making sure to put the correct sling colours into the hoist hooks. I could never remember which colour you preferred, so I'd always have to ask. The tilt of your back in the sling was crucial, and we needed the right colour to keep you comfy while I lifted you. With the mini grey remote control, I'd elevate you into the air, feeling like Darth Vader, using the Force to lift you. As you hung there helpless, I'd break into a dorky dance, singing songs about you, then I'd guide your hammocked-self over to the bed, using the control to lower you down, trying to sneak your socks off before your bom-bom hit the mattress – one less item of clothing to remove when you were bed-bound.

'Hey,' you'd say, dangling there like a monkey. 'Can't you wait until I'm on the bed to take my socks off? You're rushing, aren't you?'

'Sorry, only a little bit. I like doing it fast, like I'm working on a pit stop at the F1.'

'I know. Just makes me feel stressed sometimes. My other carers don't do it fast like this.'

I gave you a snarling look. 'Yeah, but I'm family, you piece-of-shit brother. I'll do whatever the bloody hell I want. You're under my command, you peasant. Rough care!'

You grinned. 'Oh yes, true. Rough care! I'm terribly sorry, my lord.'

Then we'd both crack up. I liked taking you by surprise, and you liked playing along.

Once you were settled on the bed, I'd unhook the sling from the hoist and slide it out from under you. Then I'd strip you down in this order: jumper, T-shirt, jogging bottoms, and finally, your pants. As I tossed each item toward the laundry basket, I'd grunt like a man on a mission. I always aimed to make you laugh during shower time, turning it into a little performance.

After stripping you bare, I'd hoist you into the shower chair and wheel you out of your bedroom. But before going straight to the bathroom, I'd slowly steer the chair toward the top of the steep staircase.

'Right, time to tackle the stairs. You ready?'

'No! Stop it!' you'd chuckle, half terrified.

'You sure? It could be fun.'

'No, please don't wheel me down the stairs, I'll die!'

You always knew I wouldn't actually tip you over the edge and send you tumbling. You trusted me. But we loved the thrill of it – the imminent danger, the what if. I never let Mum see this role-playing of ours. She wouldn't have seen the funny side of it; her eldest son, fully dressed and able-bodied, pretending to push her youngest, naked and disabled, down the stairs. Fair enough. If I was a mother, I wouldn't want to see that either.

Once in the bathroom, I'd line up your chair just right, so it fit tightly with the toilet directly underneath you. I'd hand you your URIsack and set a small plastic cup of water on the stall beside the toilet. Sometimes, I'd pretend to throw the refreshing contents of the cup at you, but I never followed through… well, apart from a couple of occasions during those hot summer days when I couldn't resist. You were a thrill-seeking teenager then, and you loved being splashed with cool water. 'Again, again, again!' you'd shout, and I'd happily oblige, refilling the cup and drenching you until we were both in stitches. After a few more giggles, I'd slip out the bathroom, leaving you to sip your water and slowly release those bowels of yours.

Sometimes, while I was waiting, I'd grab one of your hats, a pair of sunglasses, or even one of Mum's old coats – any item of clothing that wasn't mine – and throw it on. Dress-up time! Thinking it would be hilarious, and confident I'd get a laugh out of you, I'd swing open the bathroom door, strutting in with a silly accent, decked out in my makeshift costume, pretending to be someone else. Like an Australian detective or a Spanish maid. I'd chat rubbish in whatever accent I'd chosen to use, circling around, looking under the sink or behind the shower curtain, acting like I was searching for something and totally oblivious to your presence. Then, I'd walk back out onto the landing, shutting the door behind me and leaving you to your peace. I could hear you snorting with laughter as I pulled off my circus act. It made me feel like a genius. Content with my stupidity.

When you'd finished doing your tings, you'd call out my name, and I'd rush back in to clean you up···ok, not all the time. Sometimes, it would take me a sweet while – if I was reading a book, for example. I'd finish my page before diving into the clean-up of your bottylots. Bottylots! What a word. Remember how Mum would use it to describe your bom-bom? She had some great expressions. We loved them and recycled them whenever we had the opportunity. But back to your bottylots.

I'd re-enter the bathroom, wheel you out into the centre of the room, get on my hands and knees to wipe and swipe you clean. I was super-efficient at this. Quite the expert. Out of all your carers, I got the most stuck in, and you always appreciated that. I'd get right down under, like a plumber, cleaning you good and proper.

Then it was shower time. I'd get back up, push you into the corner, below the lowered-down shower head, put the brakes on, roll up my sleeves, take my socks off, and wash you down with a soft sponge, pretending I was at a car wash. I'd scrub your armpits, legs, chest, back, even behind your ears, and slide the sponge under your belly like I was swiping a credit card. I scrubbed you all over – except your privates;

you took care of them behind the curtain at the end of your shower.

I enjoyed our cleaning escapades, Sam. We had our giggles, but I always stayed diligent and on task. By the time the shower hose was turned off, you were squeaky clean, and I made sure of it.

Sometimes, if you'd requested it, I'd give you a cheeky beard shave, which I adored. Your face was a breeze to shave – so soft and smooth. Easy to glide a razor across. Mine? A rugged landscape of angles and cuts. I always ended up with nicks, especially under my chin where the hairs decided to grow in all directions. That's why I ditched the razor; a beard's less hassle. Plus, it compensates for my receding hairline and lack of head hair.

But enough about my hair woes. On this hypothetical day I'm describing to you, I wouldn't touch your beard. You liked it as you got older. Made you feel all manly and wise. So, after your scrub-down, I'd roll you back onto the bathroom mats, dry you off with your beloved *Jaws* towel, and use a less-favoured one for your shower chair, making sure to keep the metal framework from rusting.

Then, I'd wheel you back to your room, strap you in, and hoist you onto your bed. I'd sort you out with talc, foot creams, Deep Heat, deodorant, dress you in your jim-jams, slide on your night splints, and prop up your legs with the big white cushion.

After tucking you in, setting up your breathing machine, and making sure your wheelchair was on charge overnight, I'd drag your desk closer so you could reach your gadgets – iPad, iPhone, and a reading book. Then I'd give you a hug, fighting back the tears – *Why him in the mask and not me?* – say goodnight, turn off the lights, and gently close your door.

Pat on the back, Jack. Nailed it.

I know I whizzed through the last part, but I'm tired of typing and imagined caregiving. Showering you was always a long procedure – but also fun, unless we were squabbling.

I didn't know it then, but those shower routines – full of socks, slings, and silly songs – were the best part of my life.

I'm going to lean my head against the window again now – Agathe prefers the aisle seats – and have a little nap.

Sweet dreams, Sam. Sleep well.

Sweet dreams, Brother Jack.

GRIND

MONDAY 15 APRIL

I feel so miserable, Sam. Perhaps it's because I haven't had any breakfast yet. Or coffee. I'm trudging to Billy Bobs for my second week back and honestly, I cannot be bothered to teach cocky teenagers today. Strutting around like they own the place, outnumbering me like pigeons swarming a single chip. I'd rather be on holiday with you, somewhere sunny. An all-inclusive resort by the beach sounds ideal. I want to splash around in an accessible pool with you, then cut up your dinner into bite-size portions. Maybe we'd sip fruity cocktails too, watching the sun sink. Proper bromantic.

But nope. Instead, I must teach herds of children how to replicate René Magritte's pipe painting in oil paint with crusty old brushes that barely work – we've run out of fine tips, like we do with most resources. It's a shit-show waiting to happen.

I just can't even deal today. But at least you'll be there, Sam, shoulder-bound. My lucky charm. And that's a source of comfort – enough to drag me through.

In a bit, Sambit.

TUESDAY 16 APRIL

Morning, Samwise Gamgee.

You know, out of the whole jumble of nicknames I've thrown at you over the years, this one must be one of my all-time favs. Surprised I haven't used it here already, to be honest. It's got you written all over it – perfectly captures your essence, and our bond.

Growing up, I always felt like a Frodo – a dark, curly mop of hair and a permanent look of unease. And it wasn't just me who saw the resemblance. At secondary school, the other kids often called me Frodo. Compared to some of the more brutal nicknames I could mention – like *gay rabbi*, courtesy of my side curls and delicate demeanour – Frodo actually felt like a compliment. The heroic hobbit.

At Kings', I didn't have a magical ring to save them all, but I did have a heavy depression I carried everywhere like a tonne of bricks. And you, Sam, were always there to help me shoulder the load. My trusty companion. Without you, I wouldn't have made it to Mordor. You lifted me – and my burdens – as we climbed that metaphorical mountain together. Despite your weakening muscles, you were the strongest hobbit I knew – always there, listening, caring, lifting my spirits. You've always been the true hero, Samwise.

Walking to Billy Bobs this morning, I find myself reflecting on yesterday, which turned out to be surprisingly ok. I managed to teach two lessons without any drama. The suited kids even pulled off decent pipe paintings with those terrible brushes. I kept harping on about the importance of thinning out the paint with linseed oil and using just the tip of the brush to achieve subtle marks. And you know what? They listened. Not the worst day. Not the best. Comme ci, comme ça.

Now, game face on. Today's quest: food tech with a band of enthusiastic year eights. The challenge: couscous salad. Did I mention that, during the summer term, I'm forced to teach food tech at Billy Bobs? Ludicrous, really. They seem to think art teachers are jack-of-all-trades. Yes, my name's Jack – but still···

Onwards and upwards, Samwise. Up Mount Doom I go, armed with my bro, apron, and spoon.

Speak soon.

WEDNESDAY 17 APRIL

Just got back from school. I'm lying in bed alone, and I wanted to tell you that I see you every time I look at my phone. You're my screen (and life) saver. The photo I took of you at Victorious Festival two years ago – Friday 26th August 2022. Southsea Common. You and me, our first festival together. What a day.

It was absolutely scorching. As well as UV rays, we soaked up so much music. We had the best spot, right in the middle of that large accessible bay – no one in front of us to block the stage. The photo captures you smiling, sporting those black-and-white checkerboard braces of yours like you're a proud Ska musician. You're also wearing your James Blunt T-shirt you'd bought from his Royal Albert Hall gig, and your *Love Don't Hate* badge from work, to promote your company's campaign to end hate crime and celebrate diversity. You hero. Behind you, a sea of bodies sways to Primal Scream.

I love this photo because you're looking straight at me, locked in with me among all the chaos. You were genuinely happy in my company. And it was just before one of my highlights of the day – when you chatted up that pretty girl in the wheelchair. I can't remember her name – maybe you can? For now, and probably forever, we'll just call her Mystery Girl. I'd never felt such an immense pride for my younger brother as I did on that sunny day on Southsea Common.

Mystery Girl was chilling three or four metres away from us, all by herself. You liked the look of her. You said she looked *alternative*, and boyo, did she. She looked like a cool indie girl – attending a festival on her own, bobbing her head to the tunes with no shits given. She had long auburn hair and kind eyes. You thought she seemed approachable, but way out of your league. Brother Jack wasn't having any of that.

'Screw that, Sam, she's not out of your league. She's well in it. You're in the top six, she's mid table.'

You side-eyed Mystery Girl. 'She's really pretty.'

'Yeah, and so what?' I glanced at Bobby Gillespie strutting around the stage in his loud *Screamadelica* suit. I wondered if he dyed his hair. It was as dark and as full as Professor Snape's. 'So are you, Sam. You're sexy like Bobby Gillespie.'

'Who's Bobby Gillespie?'

I pointed to the singer. 'That show-off Scotsman over there. He's not that sexy, actually. Go and speak to her. You know you want to.'

'I'd like to. It would be a good step for me. I've never done it before. It could boost my confidence, couldn't it?'

'Exactly. Now or never, Sam.'

As the older brother, it was my job to egg you on. I knew how terrifying it could be to muster the courage to speak to a girl in person, especially for the first time.

Everyone needs a little push now and again, so, I nudged you with all my might. Your cheeky, hungry face told me how much you wanted to talk to Mystery Girl, but you kept talking yourself down.

'I don't know what to say to her. I don't want to make a fool out of myself. What if she has a boyfriend?'

I understood. Those same fears haunted me back in the day when my gawky younger self was trying to flirt with girls. Talking to new people, especially attractive lasses, is like jumping into a shark tank when you're introverted freakazoids like us, Sam. It's terrifying. But if you want companionship, you have to take the plunge. You knew you had to schmooze Mystery Girl – you just needed a little pep talk.

So, what you got, Brother Jack?

'You'll do just great. You're such a charmer. Such a catch. You'll probably say the wrong thing at times but who cares. That's expected. It's your first time talking to a girl. This is you practising – learning the ropes, throwing yourself into the deep end. You're not going to be perfect. No-one's first time is perfect; you'll learn through trial and error. Mistakes help you get better, right?'

Your thoughts mirrored mine, and you nodded along. You realised you were faced with a golden opportunity that day. But you'd only go on one condition: you needed to drink more alcohol first. Your Dutch courage. Fair enough, I thought. You do you, Sam. So, off you went to grab an over-priced pint of ice-cold lager from one of those pop-up bars, and I played the role of your loyal servant, lugging your plastic cup of liquid bravery to the accessible bay. Once we were settled and basking in the sun again, enjoying our VIP view, you took a sip of your drink, a mix of excitement and anxiety evident in your shaking legs and darting eyes. You were plotting your approach to Mystery Girl, still bobbing her head to Bobby G without a care in the world.

'I can do this.'

'Of course you can.'

'I think I'll just say, "Hi, do you mind if I sit next to you?"'

'She'd love that. It would make her heart melt.'

After the beer had softened your body, you finally made your move and introduced yourself. My heart pounded for you. I tried to ignore the scene, not wanting to jinx it, so I focused on Primal Scream, a band I wasn't that fussed on, but my eyes kept wandering over to you and Mystery Girl. You looked so cool, so handsome, talking with your hands and laughing. I couldn't have been a prouder brother.

About half an hour later, you swaggered back with a confident grin. I felt so pleased with myself. Master wingbrother.

'How did it go?'

'It went well. Very well.'

I fought the urge to do a victory dance – Mystery Girl was still close by. I had to play it cool, like you did. 'Yeah? That's good, Sam.'

'I asked her lots of questions.'

'Like what?'

'What music she likes. What she does for work.'

'That's amazing. What does she do then?'

'She's a journalist for magazines. She's going to write a review on Victorious Festival.'

'No way!' *Steady on, Jack, she just glanced at us. She's going to think we're weird, like I'm daring my brother to speak to her or something.* I lowered my voice. 'And you studied Journalism too. Common interests. Written in the stars. You'll have babies together soon.'

'Yeah.' You looked worn out, drunk on love.

'How're you feeling now?'

'I feel good. I want to go back and chat with her.'

'Well, of course you should. What are you waiting for?'

'Can you take me to the toilet first?' You were shaking your right leg like I did when I needed the loo.

'It would be my pleasure, kind sir.' I was your little bitch that day, and I loved it.

During our next motivational session in the cramped disabled toilet, you revealed your plan to snag Mystery Girl's number and set up a date.

'What a great bloody idea. You've got nothing to lose. I'm so happy for you, you know?'

You giggled while peeing into your URIsack, and I swatted away flies from my face. I emptied your URIsack in the grim portable loo and handed you some wet wipes for a quick clean-up. After depositing the wet wipes down the loo, you chugged down more of your now-lukewarm lager like a champ. We weren't leaving that cubicle until our conversation came to a natural halt. I felt like a football manager in the changing rooms at half-time.

'How should I ask her for her number? I've never done it before.'

'"Hey there, gorgeous! Hand over your digits so we can hook up soon."'

You snickered. 'No, really.'

'I dunno. Um, "Hey, I'd love to meet up with you sometime, can I have your number?" Something like that. Actually, no, that sounds a bit off. I don't know. Just ask her. How would *you* ask her?'

'That's just it. I don't know how.' You took another swig of beer. 'What if I say it wrong?'

'You won't. You'll find a way.' I looked around the cubicle. It smelt of hot shit and freshly cut grass. Piss stains decorated the seat. 'She's just waiting for you to make your move, Sam. Trust me – she wants you to ask her.'

'Really? You think so?'

'Definitely. She was practically drooling. And look, if I'm wrong and she's not interested, who cares. At least you gave it a go. Nothing to lose.'

'Yeah, I suppose. Nothing to lose.' You downed the dregs and tossed your cup into the loo. You little rapscallion.

'Nothing to lose. You got this.'

I swung the door open, and we exited the steam room. Pep Guardiola-talk complete. The second half awaits. Back at the disabled bay, you wasted no time going back to Mystery Girl. While I sang along to Bombay Bicycle Club, a band I was much more invested in than Primal Scream, I couldn't help but sneak glances at you two again. You were chatting her up like a stallion. Sure, there were awkward pauses – those moments of silence when you didn't know what to say – but that's just part of the game. Perfectly normal.

Yes, it was a shame that she ghosted your invite to hang out, but honestly, who cared? That was your practice round, like we'd said. You took a brave step in the right direction. You gained a ton of confidence from that encounter. Plain sailing from then on.

In your twenties, you often expressed feelings of loneliness and your desire for a girlfriend. You worried that your wheelchair would prevent you from finding love. I kept telling you to 'zip that mouth of yours, Sam, and have faith. It *will* happen.' And it did. You persevered with all those dating apps and websites – especially eHarmony – and you finally found your girl. Megan was head over heels for you. I felt like I played a part in that. You did all the hard work, of course, but I was right there, cheering you on, lifting your spirits when you faced endless swipes with zero matches.

'Sometimes it just takes a little longer. Be patient, Sam.'

'I know. It won't happen just like that.'

'Rejection's all part of the process. I've been snubbed more times than I can remember. It's just what happens. Stick in there, Samwells.'

I was desperate for you to find someone, to find companionship. To experience what it felt like to be desired. I was rooting for you the whole way. I hope that in your final moments, if you thought about me, it was as someone who championed you and encouraged you to achieve what you wanted to achieve – not the one who put you in a leg brace and made you spend Christmas in a hospital bed. I wanted you to see me as your supportive brother. Your opinion of me mattered more than you know.

***

I'm putting in a good shift at school. I need to regain my rhythm after some time off. Every lesson since you left has gone well. I'm balancing firmness with warmth, narrating the classroom in a positive way – highlighting the kids who are doing a cracking job instead of dwelling on the troublemakers. All the basic stuff. The kids are responding well to this approach, and they're producing impressive outcomes. I don't want to speak too soon, but I'm killing it.

That said, yesterday, someone stole a pot of gum right from under my desk. It happened at the end of the lesson while I was herding the kids to the gates, part of our ridiculous end-of-day ritual. It's such a flawed policy, Sam – I lead the little monsters out, leaving the last few unattended, and as I don't have the opportunity to lock the door, any old Tom, Dick, or Mohammed can wander in and take whatever they please. It's a peculiar rule, like many at Billy Bobs. This morning marked the third time my gum stash has vanished. I was fuming, hell-bent on catching the little thief. I wanted to send them straight to Guantanamo Bay for a taste of real justice. After reviewing the CCTV footage with the site team, I spotted a girl I had my suspicions about, casually leaving my room with the pot of gum and sharing it with three other teens. Unbelievable. I immediately passed the evidence to the year nine leader. I hope those scoundrels get a fair punishment. Guantanamo may be a stretch, but a day exclusion would be nice.

Not all the kids are awful, though. Some are super sweet. Like this one boy who returned a stick of charcoal he borrowed before Easter. He wrapped it up neatly in a piece of paper, all tight and secure, and handed it to me at the beginning of the lesson. Bless his cotton socks. I have to cling to the positives at old Billy Bobs.

Shower time now. I stink of BO. Not as bad as your pits, but still pretty rank. Sorry, that was uncalled for. It's just too fun to tease you on here – you can't fight back.

Muahaha!

FRIDAY 19 APRIL

I'm thinking about you less and less, Samwise. This book feels like a long, gruelling monologue, and I'm slowly accepting the fact that you're not here.

It scares me that I might forget you – your voice, your movements. The way you'd shuffle back in your chair, trying to get comfy, or how you belted out to songs with sheer oomph and gusto.

I can remember these moments, but picturing them is getting hazy, like trying to picture Grandma clearly. We only keep fragments: her posh and proper voice; her obsession with Brighton's art scene; her thick, bushy hair like Mum's. She lived alone in that big, echoey house in Wareham, with its creaking staircase and the faint smell of moth balls and dog biscuits. Dino the whippet would pad along the floorboards, weaving through rooms hung with coronation mugs and framed illustrations of Trinidadian houses. I can still hear her saying, 'So, Sam, *do* tell me all about your journalism degree,' her hand clasped on your knee during our visits.

Our memories have reduced her to a mere caricature of herself. I'm worried the same fate awaits you. Will you become a rough pencil sketch? The quiet, hairy boy who loved board games and pop hits from the noughties. The Samwise to his Baggins brother.

I hope not. You were so much more than that. It frustrates me that you're not here to remind me of all the layers of you. All I have left is my cruddy memory.

I hope I don't end up with Alzheimer's.

SATURDAY 20 APRIL

Kew Gardens today, Sam.

I'm heading there with Agathe (the Agatron, the Frenchy, the Girlfriend). We're also meeting Mum and Dad (a.k.a. The Parents or Mama J and Jamieboys). Beautiful names for beautiful people.

They're taking the M3 straight to London. I'm glad they're coming to visit their son and future fille-in-law for the day. They're trying to keep busy – filling their days with things to do, avoiding too much time alone at 12 Sidders.

Now that they're not working – they're not ready to go back just yet – they've got a lot more time on their hands. Not that you were a hassle or anything – you know what I mean. You were high maintenance. King Sam. And I was your hyperactive harlequin, always trying to entertain you, while sadness ate away at me, like in that painting by Joan Miró.

They wanted to stay the night in London to make a weekend of it, but the hotels were too expensive. Too last minute. I told them to save their overnight bags for another time – when they can book somewhere nice in advance, when the weather's better. We could walk in Walpole Park, eat at a cosy pub in Ealing, and reminisce about our Sammyboys as a family.

Ok. Finally acquiring the guts to drag myself out of bed. It's eight o'clock already.

If you were next door right now, and wanted to get up for the day, I'd leap out of my bed, ready to care for you like my life depended on it. I'd remove your breathing machine, peel off the blue tape from your nose, and take off those splints and socks so your furry legs could breathe.

After pulling out the large white cushion from under your legs, I'd wrap you in the biggest bear hug. And for a moment, I'd feel safe.

SUNDAY 21 APRIL

Let's get heavy, Sam.

You're not here anymore. I'm talking to a shadow of you. I'm talking to myself and pretending it's you.

I've often blamed your illness for my depression – and I still do – but there has to be more to it. Surely it wasn't just that my younger brother had a life-threatening illness. Pretty sure I felt off before the diagnosis hit. When exactly was that? 2008? 2009? After the teachers at Upham called home to say you and your wobbly legs should get checked out. I don't know. I'm not sure.

I don't even remember being told about your condition. No family meetings. No formal sit-downs. Maybe Mum and Dad tried to shield me from the harsh truth. Or maybe they did explain it and I blocked it out, to spare myself the inevitable pain. Maybe younger Jack was traumatised and learned to act like it never happened. Who knows? I should ask them – for my own peace of mind – but where would I even start?

Over the years, on my mission to shake off depression like it's a bad cold, doctors and therapists have asked the same questions about my childhood: *What went wrong? What caused the low moods? Why do you shrink from social situations?*

I worry whatever I say will be twisted into neat little explanations that miss the point. Sure, I got bullied. Sure, your disability was tough to accept. But maybe those weren't the real triggers? Maybe my depression and anxiety are side effects of undiagnosed ADHD. Maybe that acronym's the big bad wolf. Or maybe it's a farce – a trendy label I latched onto because it made me feel seen.

It all happened so fast. After two chats with a cheerful doctor, I walked away with a diagnosis. Was it really that obvious? Did he see the signs – or was I just playing the part? Just to clarify: I wasn't faking, Sam – you know that better than anyone. I'm hyper, impulsive, overwhelmed. I fidget, I tap, and I find making eye contact stressful. With you, I could drop the act and let my true self out, without the masks I wear around others. I did that with the doctor too – showed him who I actually am.

So yes, the symptoms were there. But they also say adults are over diagnosed with ADHD – an excuse to seem edgy and creative. Or maybe more people have it these days because there's more awareness, more acceptance. Doctors understand it better. What looks like 'overdiagnosis' is the aftershock of years of underdiagnosis.

I can't say for certain if I was misdiagnosed. It's just that it unfolded so fast, like the professionals told me what I wanted to hear – gave me an answer to my problems. But my problems persist. Maybe I need to wait for the medication. But what if they throw a wrench in the works, especially if I don't truly have ADHD? And what if they react badly to the anti-depressants I'm on?

Arghh. Who the hell knows, Sam?

I walk around with invisible scars while everyone assumes I'm peachy because I don't spill my guts. I put on a show, smile like a clown, juggle life – organising your funeral party, working a demanding job, trying to keep my fiancée happy. But inside? I'm a crumbling mess, more fragile than the most fragile little kids in my class.

I'm shy. I crave my own space. I do everything I can just to stay afloat.

They say if you need help, you should scream out. Well, this is me screaming. I'm on meds. I'm getting therapy. I'm finally telling people I'm a depressive with ADHD. Maybe those labels explain my moods. Maybe they don't. Either way, they give me a language – a way to show the world why I retreat, why my social battery dies.

Is it helping? Dumping like that. Maybe. It helps me accept myself more than before, instead of hiding behind the act. And that's something.

THE OTHER LEG DAY

MONDAY 22 APRIL

Happy Monday, Sam.

I'm trudging up this never-ending hill on my way to Billy Bobs. The rising sun's warming my freshly shaven head. Proper skinhead these days. Like *This is England*. Grade 0 all over. Trying to hide my receding hairline.

I've figured my commute is the best time to talk to you. No distractions. Just me, a hill, and the ghost of my brother.

Speaking of ghosts, your WhatsApp's still here, but your display picture is gone. Now you're just a blank white head on a grey background. Ghostly. Is your digital presence fading too? Hope not.

A scene keeps looping in my head lately – the other leg day. Family holiday in North Wales. Snowdonia, 2017. We were in a Premier Inn in Bangor. You and I had one room. Mum and Dad had the other.

The Bangor Brothers, in their bedroom with their two single beds, a walk-in shower, and a big wall-mounted TV, were squabbling, as they often did back then. It had something to do with the TV. Something trivial. I said something you didn't like. I can't remember the exact words, only the feeling: you didn't like what came out of my mouth.

That happened a lot in your teens and early twenties. Certain words or phrases set you off. You only took it out on me and The Parents. If a carer said the same thing, you wouldn't react. But with us, you made your feelings known. You'd interrogate us like we were on trial. Sometimes you'd throw things in frustration, like shampoo bottles or cutlery. But during that trip in Wales, you took it to another level.

Instead of throwing an inanimate object, you decided to throw *yourself.*

I was in the middle of changing you after your evening shower. We were picking something on TV to have on in the background. I said something you didn't appreciate – something like, 'Oh, just pop anything on, Sam' – and you reacted.

You slid off the bed. Deliberately.

You knew what it meant. You knew I'd have to lift you from the floor, causing a lot of pain for both of us. You did it as a statement. A sharp, little way to express your annoyance.

Deal with this, Jack, you prick.

It was impulsive, reckless, and you fractured your right leg because of the fall.

It wasn't my fault. An argument doesn't mean a leg should break. I shouldn't have had to bear the blame for that, but I did. The guilt weighed heavily on me.

I can't control your temper, and I definitely couldn't control it back then.

You had to go to sleep with that fracture. We thought it was just a bruise. You'd never broken your leg before, so it didn't even cross our minds. Lucky for us, it was the last night of the holiday, and we were driving back to Hampshire the next day.

But it shouldn't have happened, Sam. You didn't need harm yourself like that. You felt compelled to. A moment of mad desperation. Your cry for help.

A few weeks later, you finally reached out to the NHS. It took an eternity, but you got your counselling. You learned how to manage your rage. You dove into self-help books and chanted daily affirmations like a mantra. You made a serious effort to improve. And it worked. You levelled up. You never self-harmed like that again. Bravo, Sam, bravo.

Popping into Tesco now for a meal deal. What a thrilling life I lead.

***

Meal deal in the bag. Right – the right leg.

The regret you carried. How totally avoidable it was. How your temper got the best of you.

You had some serious anger in you, Sammyboys. There were moments when you didn't consider the consequences of your actions. I think I get why.

Living in a wheelchair must've been relentless. You couldn't just *do* things. You constantly had to negotiate with everyone – including me, in that hotel room. You had to sit there on the edge of the bed, waiting for me to help you into your jim-jams. You couldn't manage it on your own. And you couldn't have a shower without me there. You couldn't have any privacy. You had to be so patient with everyone. No wonder you blew up when someone asked you to change channel.

In a way, I'm glad it happened with me there instead of The Parents. I wouldn't want them to carry that weight. Though maybe they'd have handled it differently, not feeling as accountable as I did. Maybe they'd have thought it was karma biting you in the bottylots.

Still – I can't shake the fact that both times you fractured your leg, I was present. Am I the problem? How furious you must've been, launching yourself onto the floor over something I said.

Maybe it was because we were close. Bangor Brothers. And you felt free to let loose around me?

You often said I was refreshingly honest – unlike others who tiptoed around your feelings – and sometimes that honesty stung. I guess you thought I could take your anger. I don't know, Sam.

I think about those fractured legs more than I should. Maybe it's time to accept that neither incident was really my fault. One stemmed from your frustration, the other from my clumsiness. Are we even now? Not that it matters.

You're somewhere else, and I'm still climbing hills, watching the sun play hide and seek with the clouds, bracing myself for another Billy Bobs shit show.

The technician's off this week after a tumble at the supermarket while shopping for the Food Tech supplies – talk about irony. The poor woman deserves a break. But the art department relies heavily on her. The curriculum's demanding, and there are teachers galore here. She's responsible for prepping resources and setting up the practical lessons, so it's up to us teachers to pitch in this week.

I've got an acrylic painting class with Year 9, then Food Tech with Year 8. Never taught Food Tech before. Usually the technician would be there, but today it's just Mr. Waddington and thirty youngens with sharp objects and mixed emotions.

Wish me luck. No – it's all fine. I'm good with the kids.

Just to reiterate: no one's at fault for those fractures. Can we agree on that?

I'm at the school gate now. Wish I could U–turn and head home, but bills don't pay themselves. London isn't cheap.

Speak soon, brother.

***

Home now, Sam. I'm slumped on the sofa, staring at the kettle I boiled five minutes ago, willing the cardamom tea to make itself. I should get off my fat arse, but the cushy nest has claimed me.

During a cover lesson today – I'm occasionally put on cover when another teacher's sick – I casually mentioned to some Year 11s that you'd died. Can't remember why it came up. Just did.

This enthusiastic kid wouldn't stop firing questions at me. Very direct, no filter.

'Do you visit your brother's grave every day, Sir?'

I couldn't help but chuckle while I pretended to busy myself on my laptop. 'Well, he hasn't really been buried, so not really.'

'Where is he then?'

'Good question. He's at the funeral directors, I guess. The Chapel of Rest, they call it. He was cremated.'

I was candid with him, just like he was with me. I don't mind discussing your absence. Death's part of life, right? He asked about your disability, and I laid it out.

'People with Duchenne usually don't stick around past their thirties. They have a limited lifespan.'

'That's really sad, Sir.'

He wasn't wrong.

Most of these kids have no idea disabilities like yours exist, Sam. Billy Bobs doesn't have a single wheelchair in sight – and forget about lifts. I can only imagine what they think about wheelchair users. Teachers never bring it up, probably not a dinner-table topic either. And there's not a lot of representation in the media. There's growing representation around race and sexuality – which is great –

but physical disability still feels invisible. These kids are growing up in a wheelchair-free bubble.

Some of them, I bet, have never seen another teen on wheels. But they exist, don't they? Hundreds of thousands of boys with Duchenne, just like you, roaming the planet. And that's just one of the many physical disabilities that put young people in chairs. It's important to recognise these people, to acknowledge their presence.

'Oh, look, A person in a wheelchair. They're real. They're a teenager like me, but with wheels.'

I'll do my best to get this book out there, Sam. To showcase *you*. To inform. To remind people of all the brilliant, complex, funny, extraordinary young men like you. Special souls who live fully – and leave us far too soon.

I need to reboil the kettle.

A bientôt.

SHITTY MCVITIE

SATURDAY 27 APRIL (MORNING)

Cried in the shower again, Sam. Keeps happening. I think being surrounded by water might activate the tears?

While scrubbing my hairy pits, I remembered you visiting me for the day in London. You never got the chance to see where I lived – the places I called home. The flat in Canada Water, the one in Barons Court, the three in Camberwell, and now this one in Ealing.

I've moved around a lot here, and those little flats were always a mystery to you.

I would've loved to cook you some dindins. Have you stay the night. But none of my home–away–from–homes had step–free access or lifts to my floor, and even if they did, you couldn't have stayed – no hoist, no sling, no walk–in shower or shower chair. You would've had to sleep in your chair.

So whenever you visited, we always ended up in Central London, which was enjoyable, don't get me wrong, but I wanted more. I wanted to host you for a night or two, so we could spend the whole weekend together. We could roam the streets in the evening, go to the West End, enjoy a fancy dinner somewhere, and indulge in a hearty fry up the next morning. An absolute dream.

Our daytime outings in the metropolis always felt hurried. London isn't built for wheelchairs, not really. Moving from one crowded place to another took a lot of time and careful planning. You'd have to leave early in the afternoon because you'd be worn out, which was understandable – Central can suck the energy out of you. Tube journeys were especially tiring, as we had to ensure we got on and off at step-free stations, which aren't very common – albeit better than other cities like Paris. Finding those platform humps that allow flat access so we could board the train – and then squeezing a wheelchair onto a packed tube during rush hour – was such a kerfuffle. How you didn't bump into anyone was beyond me. Master navigator.

Perhaps I underestimated how exhausting it would be for you. I just wanted you to enjoy a day out in London with your big bro, and I knew you wanted that too. You loved consuming the big cities. Berlin, Manchester, New York etc. Dining out, shopping, and going to concerts or theatre shows put you on cloud nine.

Duchenne had its claws on you, Sam, but you never let that evil bastard hold you back. You dragged it along with you like a pesky pet, determined to make the most of every day. That's why you kept coming to London to see me and soak up the sights. Your stubbornness was impressive, just like many other brave young men in wheelchairs. I loved seeing that side of you, pushing your way onto a tube carriage, even if it meant saying, 'Sorry, excuse me,' over and over. You trooper.

Sometimes you'd come for the afternoon and go back in the evening. I remember when we took the Jubilee Line from Waterloo to Bond Street to enjoy some live classical music at Wigmore Hall. We listened to a balding pianist perform some of Chopin's *Nocturnes*. They were special, weren't they? – moody and stripped down. We sat at the back, quietly enjoying the music like all the other smartly dressed folk, digesting the steak and chips we had earlier.

'Not bad, this old geezer, is he, Sam?' I whispered in a dodgy cockney accent.

You snickered. 'Nah, he ain't bad at all, mate.'

After the concert, we rushed back to the tube to ensure you caught your evening train to Beastly Eastleigh at Waterloo. We made it by the skin of our teeth that night.

We always got there in the end. I made sure to ask the guard for the ramp for you, and once you were safely on the train, settled in the wheelchair area with your travelling essentials to hand – iPhone, toilet bag with your Urisack and wet wipes, water bottle, book, wallet, etc., I gave you a big bruvhug and said, 'Text me when you're home, ok?'

And then the bit I hated most. Waving goodbye from the platform, trying to keep my emotions in check while you waved back, but once the train pulled away, the tears escaped. I hated leaving you behind. I felt a tremendous sense of guilt. It was hard for you to visit me, and I wished you could come inside my flat and stay over. Living so far away from you felt wrong. I'd see you through the window, sitting near the doors, so exposed next to the toilet and bike rack, without the privacy others had. Even when you got home, you had little privacy because someone had to help you with everything. There were always people around you. What was it like, constantly interacting with others?

I hated standing on that Waterloo platform and watching you leave. I wanted to stay with you a bit longer, give you anuva bruvhug or two. Tell you how proud I was of you. I'd walk to the barriers, letting the tears fall like a toddler who lost their favourite toy, and then dry my eyes as I tubed it back to Canada Water, to Camberwell, to Hammersmith, or to Ealing – wherever I was living then. Back to my London life.

I felt ashamed, like I was abandoning a brother in need.

***

Hey, again – second lil message of the day.

Earlier, while I was lying in bed listening to a rocksteady playlist, the smooth basslines of 'I'm Still in Love' by Alton Ellis mingling with my heartbeat, I found myself mindlessly scrolling through photos on my phone.

I stumbled upon one of you sitting next to Grandad's coffin – from our visit to the Chapel of Rest in Winchester last year.

The Parents stayed outside. Mum had already been in, and Dad couldn't bear to see a wicker casket, knowing his father was inside.

The Waddington Brothers, however, went in – mainly for you, Samwise. You were eager to see Grandad. Unlike the rest of us, your moments with him were few before he slipped away.

The house where he and Granny lived was out of reach – too many steps. Grandad felt the weight of it too, knowing his youngest Waddington couldn't visit him in his own home.

That house, a relic of his move from Staffordshire to Hampshire in the late seventies, held memories of Granny, three children – Suzanne, Carolyn, and our future dad, Jamieboys – and a handful of suitcases, as he began his role as an officer at Winchester Prison. A fresh start down south.

Over the years, the family grew, and so did the memories. Grandchildren, great-grandchildren. Parties, get togethers. It became a sanctuary.

It wasn't Grandad's fault you couldn't enter; how could he foresee having a grandchild in a wheelchair? Nor was it yours, Sam. Douchebag Duchenne again, casting its shadow.

We took some photos in the Chapel of Rest. You next to our Grandad's casket, gazing solemnly at the spot where his head lay, your hand perched on the edge of the wicker.

That picture was taken in August 2023. Little did you know you'd soon find yourself in a dark box just like his, waiting for visitors to pay their respects.

Cruelty.

TUESDAY 30 APRIL (MORNING)

Feel like a shitty McVitie today, Samwells. A sad, crumbling biscuit.

Am I just exploiting you and your youness to write this book? Am I milking your story for a taste of fame? Is that what all these sombre words are about?

No. I'm not cashing in on you and your struggles.

I think I'm just desperate to share it. I need to talk about you. There's too much to keep bottled up.

Speaking of cash, I just paid the deposit for our wedding photographer. It's happening, Sam. Saturday, 25th May. A fancy stately home near Winchester called Houghton Lodge. We found the place online and fell in love with it on our first visit.

I've also paid my share of the rent. Over a grand has fucked off from my account, just like that, on my tube ride to work.

But hey, tomorrow's payday. Good old reliable Billy Bobs.

TUESDAY 30 APRIL (EVENING)

Sifting through your endless lists and grand plans on your iCloud is hard work. You knew your days were limited, and you were so intent on filling them with memories, as if trying to outrun the clock – tribute acts (hello, Jive Talkin' and Fastlove), plays (wassup, *The Kite Runner*), concerts (howdy, James Blunt), Q&As with your favourite celebrities (what u sayin, Brian Cox).

I wish I'd been more proactive in booking the events you wanted to attend but felt you had no one to accompany you. You didn't always want to go on your own with your carers; you wanted friends or family by your side. I regret not being your plus-one more often.

There are many things I wish I'd done differently, and every word I write drags up the ghosts of what could've been. This love-letter-writing exercise isn't doing my sanity any favours; it's pouring salt in an open wound.

That's why I've decided to hit pause on this correspondence. Turns out I'm not as resilient as I thought. The strength you lent me is dwindling. I'm running low on my metaphorical spinach, feeling like a wilted leaf.

My eyes are straining from this blinding white screen, and I'm neglecting my general health – letting Agathe's five-star meals go cold while I write to you is a biggie. I'm becoming more withdrawn and anxious, forgetting to exercise, speak to friends, do the cleaning.

Plus, I really need to start applying to new schools. A change of scenery might be the magic potion your brother needs. And let's be honest, I don't half complain about Billy Bobs. Surely that's a sign.

I'm hiding behind this book, and it's having a negative effect on me. I know it won't always be like this. Eventually, it'll turn into a cathartic voyage of self-discovery – or something equally dramatic. But there's no need to sprint; I should take it easy. Pace myself. Trust the process.

Maybe I won't write every day like I've been doing.

As I'm jotting this down, Agathe's opening the front door. She's returned from the bureau – two days a week in the land of cubicles, the rest in our cosy, little Victorian flat. She must be wiped out.

Time to spend some time with my future wifey.

Speak soon, Sam.

SPINACH

WEDNESDAY 1 MAY

Screw it. Couldn't resist. Jack's back. Maybe there's a likkle bit of spinach left, after all. That little hiatus? Not really a break. But now I'm back with fresh vigour. What I said yesterday was true – but too extreme. I can keep writing to you. I have to. This is my therapy session with a friendly ghost.

I'll just pick my moments wisely – definitely not when Agathe's around, or when she's cooking for me. I'll remember to eat. To exercise. Writing to you won't take precedence over my basic needs. And I'll try to rein it in when it comes to slagging myself off. It's doable.

You're my therapist, Sam. I said that in the first message on the train, didn't I? I need to get my thoughts out before I can even think about *moving on* – a grief phrase I can't stand. This is part of my healing. It helps me grapple with what happened to you, helps me make sense of the turmoil. I'll keep at it, but I won't let it consume me. I'll aim for moderation.

Forgot to tell you – The Parents covered your funeral party expenses yesterday. I transferred three grand from your account to help. You basically contributed to your own funeral party. How messed up is that? But I know you'd understand. Your money had to go somewhere, right? And funerals cost an arm and a leg.

I've been mulling over whether you ever thought about it. You knew you were going to die young – did you ever ponder the details of your funeral? The logistics? Who'd pay for it? Where would your money end up? I'm guessing you didn't. Your focus was on bucket-list ticking and living life to the max.

I've been thinking about your funeral for years. Back when I was a teenager, teachers would ask about my future ambitions, and my mind always drifted to you – how and when you'd die, how and when I'd be brotherless. Samless. I envisioned myself planning your funeral party, tears streaming down my proud face as your coffin sank into the earth. I always pictured a burial, not cremation. But I never told the nosy teachers any of this. Can you imagine their faces? If a kid told me something like that at Billy Bobs, I'd be speechless. What the hell would I say? That's why I kept those morbid musings to myself. After swiping them from my juvenile mind, I'd offer an upbeat, ambitious response, claiming I'd be a wildly successful artist. Jacko Picasso.

Jacko Picasso-in-the-making often found himself overshadowed by Jacko the non-disabled sibling of Samo – whose death was waiting around the bend. These thoughts haunted me like a persistent nightmare: your upcoming death, the decline of your body, the pain it would inflict on me. The shame of being the sibling who survived felt unbearable. You'd die, I'd remain. I was the lucky one – but did I deserve it?

I'm managing better now, but the shame persists. Especially because your death is real now. I feel uneasy in my own skin. It's awkward speaking to Mama J and Jamieboys. I feel like a living reminder of their lost child. I survived. You didn't. Sometimes I feel like I'm in their way – like they'd rather you be here instead. I know it's not true, but we can't always be rational, can we?

The big-dog irrational thought that gnaws at me is the sense of responsibility for your passing. I was the firstborn. Those DMD genes could've easily been mine. But if I follow that line of reasoning, then Mum would be to blame for passing the genes to you. Or Grandma for handing them down to her? And that's absurd, isn't it? How can they be held accountable? It's equally absurd to think I caused your death. I loved you. I didn't redrum you.

FRIDAY 3 MAY

Back home today, Sam. I came to visit Mama J and Jamieboys for the bank holiday weekend.

As soon as I arrived, I jumped straight in the shower to wash away all that London grime. When I stepped out, dripping and dazed, I realised I hadn't checked if there was a towel waiting. Typical. So, without thinking, I padded into your room to grab one from the cupboard.

Your scent still lingers. I think most of it comes from your chair, so I took a good whiff, especially near the headrest. I was right: that hair grease was the source. I hugged your seat on wheels – butt-naked – leaving a ghostly gap with my arms where your body used to be. It felt like a warm hug from the past.

Back in the bathroom, I noticed your pubes scattered around the corners of the room, and I started to cry. Those little curls really knew how to spread, didn't they? Your steroid-fuelled hair growth left its mark. I never want that bathroom floor hoovered. Never ever. Seeing your rogue hairs brings me comfort – like a cat owner cherishing the fur.

But 12 Sidders will change. Of course it will. The lift will go, along with your chair, your shower chair, your pubes, and even your bed. Your smell will fade too, Sam. I thought about all this in the shower. The removal of your things feels like another farewell. Those assistive technologies were part of you. Extended limbs. Like you were part machine. Like you were Darth Vader – I've used that simile already, haven't I? Oh well. Sam the Sith. I like it. It's got a ring to it.

After my shower, I dragged myself downstairs. Mum was curled up in the corner of the sofa, eyes glued to the TV, pretending the screen could absorb her sorrow. Her gaze was vacant. She looked lost and in need of a hug, so I shuffled over. She clocked my puffy, red face, and we consoled each other – two emotional wrecks. Not as adept at holding it together as Dad.

Life at 12 Sidders feels off without you, Sam. I miss the sound of your wheelchair rolling through the house. The clicks and clanks of the mechanics when you stop-started or adjusted a setting. The slow *beep beep* when you powered on and off. The low hum as you moved between floors. Those sounds were my comfort. Now there's this unsettling silence. It's even tougher for Mum and Dad. They're stuck with it.

I keep spotting the funeral party brochures I designed for you. They're scattered around the house. Mum has turned 12 Sidders into a shrine – candles flickering beside folded brochures on mantelpieces. It's a thoughtful gesture, but also a loud reminder that you're gone. And now we're left with nothing but cartridge paper from Vistaprint. Not sure how to process that.

I do, however, enjoy seeing you in that navy-blue suit and bow tie on the front cover. I used the photo from your Norwegian cruise with The Parents – I wish I'd joined you on that bonanza, but I was off backpacking in the Balkans with Agathe. I wish I could've been there for your karaoke sesh with Alex, your carer at the time. I saw the video Mum took while lazing on a crowded beach in Split, but being there on the big boat, clapping along – that would've been amazing.

You belted out '(I've Had) The Time of My Life' to pretty much the whole boat. Whizzing around the stage, glancing back at the lyrics on screen now and then. You and Alex were a hit, Sam.

You'd be so proud of her, by the way, she's making her professional stage debut in *Starlight Express* this June. Pretty incredible, right? I'm sure you'll be cheering her on from the stars.

***

I wish I hugged you more when you were alive.

Over the years, I noticed how hesitant people were to hug you. In social situations, they'd hug me and not you, opting for a wave or a gentle pat on your shoulder instead. Not everyone, don't get me wrong – close family always hugged you – but others seemed unsure, uncomfortable.

Where do I start? I don't want to hurt him. Do I stand in front or to the side of him? How should I wrap my arms around him? One arm or two? How far do I lean down – do I squat, or just bend forward? Do I hug just his body or part of the chair too? Where do I put my head – above, below, or beside his?

They probably avoided hugging you, Sam, as it involved too much brain power – and they didn't want to look foolish.

It always made me feel for you, though. There I was, getting a hug, while you sat there empty-handed. 'Hey, he's here too,' I wanted to say.

You couldn't initiate hugs. You couldn't exactly ask for one. You had to rely on others to approach you. And while you were hugged, it wasn't as often as I wished. I wanted you to be showered in them.

But did it matter what I wanted? How did you feel about the hug drought? Did it bother you? I guess I'll never know. We rarely spoke about hugging, did we?

When we were younger, I didn't think twice, you know. I'd hop onto your chair and wrap my arms and legs around you like a gibbon. It was instinctive. But as we got older, things changed. We transitioned into adulthood and became more reserved. Suddenly, your chair felt like a boundary – a little bubble, your protective shell. I didn't want to invade your space the way I used to.

Still, I made sure to give you a hearty hug when I said hi or bye. And I always hugged you at bedtime. That was easier – you were lying down. I'd rest my head on your chest and soak in your warmth.

But in the chair, it was different. Too many poky bits of plastic and metal. And I doubted you wanted a thirty-year-old man monkey-climbing onto you anymore. With your arms too weak to hug back, it complicated things. Lifting them just to wrap around me was exhausting for you. When I did hug you, I was always careful not to squeeze too tightly, knowing how easily you bruised.

The hugs dwindled over the years. But now? Now I want nothing more than to give you the biggest, squeeziest, warmest, monkeyist of hugs I can muster. Enough to open a whole tin of cartoon spinach.

HI JACK

Hi Jack.

I'm hijacking your novel. To show you that I'm part of your memoir. I'm writing the way you do, with short, snappy sentences.

Writing through you. Through your thumb tapping on your iPhone screen. I'm also floating in my bedroom, watching Dad dig through my collectables to remind himself of my little quirks. He's in his jim-jams, smiling. I can be anywhere, anytime, which is really strange. I like how you picture me as a tiny version of myself, like one of the children in *Honey, I Shrunk the Kids*.

Dad's rummaging through my shiny key rings, the ones dangling off my chest of drawers. He's talking to you as he noses around, listing them out loud so you can hear. You're sprawled in your bed, quietly listening to one of your favourite Van Morrison albums, *Poetic Champions Compose,* on your phone. I know everything!

'Here's the one from Croatia. You gave him that one, Jack. From your holiday in the Balkans.'

'Oh yeah, I remember buying that for him at a little souvenir shop. In Zagreb, I think.'

'The ABBA one's nice too. Black and white. That's from when he went with you, wasn't it? In London.'

'Yeah, he loved that one. He spent about fifty pounds on ABBA souvenirs that day. Shopkeeper's dream, he is, Dad.'

'Ah, bless him. Oh, I like his Lionel Richie one. When he went with Mum in Romsey.'

He's not missing any one of them, Jack. He loves telling people all the details, doesn't he? Like how he calls Granny in the evenings to recount every ingredient from his lunch. *Cheese on toast with Worcestershire sauce. A side salad. Diced radishes and cucumber⋯* We used to poke fun at him for it. Mum was the main culprit. She'd pretend to yawn when he filled Granny in on his day. That always cracked us up.

Dad's lost in nostalgia, looking at all my things, like when you read my diaries and notepads. My handwriting makes you smile. The way I craft my sentences gets you laughing. Like what I penned on July 5th, 2024: *ONE YEAR ON – GRANDAD DEATH.* You like how blunt it sounds. I love how it tickles your funny bone.

Feel free to take my diaries back to London – every single one of them: 2024, 2023, 2022, and 2021. They're yours now, just like my lists. Flip through the pages and enjoy my bold, confident scrawl. I can see it helps you.

Keep sharing them here; I love reliving those moments, and I know you do too. Do whatever you need to feel better.

Dad texts me every morning on WhatsApp. Typical Dad messages, full of his usual cheer, punctuated with exclamation marks and kisses at the end. He loves to share his daily plans, always eager to keep me in the loop.

Meanwhile, Mum showers my room with a hundred kisses every night and strolls through Marwell Zoo the next day, thinking of me. Tell Mum thanks for stroking my head during my final moments. Lovely parents, I have.

And here you are, writing your memoir, chatting with me, reminiscing. Keep at it, Jack. You really are talented – so much more than just a teacher. I know you are. You're the most creative person I know. You've got style and talent. My artistic older brother, you're remarkable.

It's ok to feel sad. You're allowed to cry. Let it out; it's healthy. But don't get stuck in your sadness. I know it's tempting to stay sad and angry all the time – it's what you're used to. But in the long run, it'll only weigh you down more and zap your energy. I don't like seeing you so gloomy. I prefer seeing you laughing, being playful, and embracing your silly side. You used to love being goofy around me. You felt at ease, lifting my spirits, and I cherished those times. Like when you'd call after work, slipping into a thick Yorkshire or Liverpudlian accent, testing out jokes, gossiping about football. You think you've lost that relationship with me – your favourite one – but you haven't. Just because I'm not there physically doesn't mean you can't still be the same with me in spirit. Every time I catch you doing your funny voices or bizarre zombie walks around your flat, I wish you could see me smiling. You're still making me laugh, my hilarious bro. Keep lollygagging. But not too often. Especially around Agathe. Don't push her buttons. I'm sure she doesn't appreciate you singing football chants first thing in the morning. Save those songs for me when she's not around.

There's so much I like seeing you do, and I want front-row seats. I like seeing you go about your life. Pushing yourself to go to the pub with your colleagues after work. Ordering lemonade while they're swigging beers. Not feeling the need to drink alcohol – your little act of social rebellion. Planning your wedding and trip to Singypoors and Indonesia with Agathe, as well as the pilgrimage to the summit of the Ben! Running around frantically at work, trying to prep for your next lesson. Writing your book about me with enthusiasm. Listening to new music and forming opinions on it. How good Arlo Parks and Porridge Radio are. Buying pins and building your pin board collection. Shaving your head and trimming your beard every couple of days to look neat and clean – straight edge, but not really. Looking in the mirror and caring about your appearance. Going out to restaurants with The Agatron. Parks Kitchen, the best Korean in town. Exercising and drinking plenty of water. Trying to live. I like you living.

I understand that you feel bad for me, but really, it's fine. I've come to terms with not being around physically. And I adapted to my disability pretty quickly; it's all I've ever known. I didn't feel sorry for myself. Sure, there were tough times, but I just rolled with the punches and found ways to cope. No need to measure yourself against my experiences. You've got your monsters, and you need to hug them. Embrace who you are, Jack. I know self-love's a challenge for you. You often feel like you're doing the wrong thing, getting in the way, being a ham-fisted nuisance. And you can't stop blaming yourself for my broken leg(s). But it doesn't matter how it happened. And that's coming from me, the king of overanalysing, getting to the bottom of things; the why, the what, the when's, the how's. But I really don't care anymore. Living with broken legs was tough, but I was used to facing challenges – I came to expect them. It bothered me less than it bothered you if that makes sense. You've got nothing to apologise for.

But I know you. You'll keep feeling sorry for me, and I guess that's normal for someone in your position. I can't truly grasp what it was like having a younger brother with a disability. It must've been challenging growing up with me – putting on my clothes and playing football on your own in the garden. Feeling tormented by your privileges. Feeling guilty for being able to walk. But I do know what it's like to have an older brother wrestling with underlying depression. It used to sting seeing you upset. Still does. Watching you cry and beat yourself up. You have no need to be so critical of yourself. You're doing you just fine.

You've achieved so much, and I'm so proud of my older brother. You face your fears and stage fright every weekday by standing up and teaching. You're getting married next year, and soon you'll be knee-deep in diaper duties. You're going to be a great husband and dad, just like our Jamieboys. You're doing wonderfully. I want to see you smile at yourself in the mirror when you shave that head and oil that beard. I want you to give yourself virtual hugs – if I had arms with enough strength in them, I'd give you a big grizzly bear hug, but I'm just an invisible thingamajig, a memory that floats in the minds of others. That's why I can show up anywhere, anytime. When enough people think of me, I duplicate and merge all my selves together and I become this huge cloud-type thing, or a murmuration of birds. Life after death is surreal. You'd say, 'Wow. Bloody hell, Sam. That's something else.' You do love your *wows*, like a child in wonder. Find that wonder. Keep wowing.

I can see you're tired now. Go rest those eyes and give your thumb a break. If nightmares creep in, treat them like a good old horror flick that you've written, directed, and starred in.

Night, Jack. Brother Jack.

SATURDAY 5 MAY

Thanks for hijacking my novel the other day, Sam, you creepy little crab. No, it was a solid read – and you were spot on about everything.

I'm trying to sell your wheelchair. The mighty Permobil. The M3 Corpus. Sounds like a gun. A deadly weapon. Or a corpse. Every time I type it out for ads and emails, I'm brought back to that dreadful Sunday night when you were, well, a corpse.

I've posted ads on Facebook Marketplace, Gumtree, and eBay. So far, the only response I've received is from a 'woman' on Facebook Marketplace. 'She' has two photos, two friends, and zero posts. The profile was created this year. Great! But seriously – who in their right mind asks about a wheelchair with zero intention of buying it? Looks like selling your Corpus might take a while.

This morning, I thought about adding more information to the ads – specs, dimensions, all that jazz. But I just couldn't bring myself to grab a tape measure and start measuring after spending so long on ad-writing. I needed a break.

After breakfast avec The Parents, I opened your Notes app on iCloud, which I browse through about once a week for shits and gigs. I scrolled to the bottom, where I rarely venture as you have so many bloody notes, and guess what I found? A note titled – drum roll, please – *Permobil M3 Corpus Dimensions*. Madness. It had all the relevant deets: length, width, height, weight of your chair. Like you'd read my mind, Sammyboys.

Maybe you are in fact part of this memoir. Guiding me to your Notes app to save me from measuring. I never liked tape measures: too long and snappy.

WEDNESDAY 8 MAY

It's a balmy twenty-two degrees, and my phone's heating up like a hot brick. I'm at the tube station near Billy Bobs, lounging on a bench at the far end of the platform, basking in the sun. My train to Ealing Common's due in ten minutes. Time for a daily update, Samwise.

Work was a whirlwind, but I survived. The kids churned out some decent little creations.

Key Stage 3 were sharpening their pencils and observational drawing skills, while the GCSE crew took real pride in their coursework – refining their lively portraits in the expressive, impasto style of Françoise Neilly. Squinting, tweaking. All hunky-dory.

During my lunch break – while I was on the bog, of all places – I imagined you dead on your bed. No idea why it popped into my head. Grief really does come in waves. The moment a poo plopped into the loo, I thought about a rather dead you. No twitching, no movement. Just you lying there, with the defibrillator's imprint still fresh on your chest. I could almost feel the grooves where the machine tried to zap you back to life. Back to dinner downstairs with Mum, Dad, and Megan. Back to evening TV and chinwags. But it wasn't to be.

Y ou had a shopping list of dreams. So many things left unticked. But in that moment, with Death winking at you, your perspective shifted. You saw it all, didn't you? What you'd done. What you'd made of your life. It brought you peace.

You left on high note, Sam. Going out in style, like the main character you always were. Everything was in place. And you knew it. No more Duchenne to wrestle with.

That minute or so before you left, it was just you, your grin, and your treasure trove of memories. Off you floated. A weight off your muscles.

NOTING

THURSDAY 9 MAY

I know I'll have to wrap up this book eventually, and the thought of it is daunting. Feels like I'm bidding you adieu, even though our heart-to-hearts will continue in my mind. I just won't be writing to you as often, and that's hard for me to accept. I want to keep our written banter alive, but I can't keep this up forever. When I put down that final full stop, it'll mark the end of our written exchanges. Let's call it a *pause* instead of a definitive *end* as I'm sure I'll write something else or find another way to communicate with you. I'll work it out. Still, it's a big deal – a big, overwhelming full stop. A big black hole. Maybe I should end this book with a comma instead? Or an ellipsis? To be continued⋯

Is that too sentimental? This whole book is a sentimental slodge, to be fair. As King Robert Smith of The Cure crooned to his elder brother who passed away recently, 'I can never say goodbye.'

FRIDAY 10 MAY (MORNING)

On my journey to work again, Sam. I like this time of day. Me n' you, no one else.

The heat's still clinging on. Not complaining. Love a bitta warmth. I slathered on sunscreen before leaving the flat, and now I smell like holidays. Remember those? Cyprus, Trinny, Florida. Good times.

I'm seeing Megan this afternoon after work. Yes, you heard that right. We're meeting near Waterloo – a nice halfway point. We never did manage that double date in London, did we? You, Megan, me, Agathe. But we had one in Soton, thanks to Cheerful Charlie, your carer at the time, who drove us. We had pizza at this new Italian restaurant. We were sat next to our girlfriends and I couldn't have been happier. If your leg hadn't snapped, maybe we'd have had more of those meals. You'd have come to London with your Essex girl, and wined and dined with me and my French femme. Tickety-boo.

Today, it's just me and Megan. It'll feel strange without you. I got used to seeing you two together – hard to miss that vibrant duo. Megan in her neon coats and blue dreads, you bundled in your chair, fighting off the chills with a beanie, scarf, and that pug-print throw you couldn't leave the house without. You two always looked like a moving art installation. Always made me smile.

I want to make sure she's ok – for my own peace of mind. That night in March must've been a nightmare for her. While Mum and Dad, the neighbours, and the doctors were scrambling, Megan hid in my old room – the one she always used when visiting. I can't even imagine what she heard···

and what she didn't. Everyone's voice but yours. I wish she hadn't been there that weekend, Sammyboys, but in a twisted way, I'm grateful she was. She stayed to the end – your girlfriend, the one you were head over heels for.

If only your big bro had been there too. Just imagine. Part of me thinks you let me off easy by sparing me the sight of you struggling for your last breath.

I wasn't there that weekend, Sam. Maybe that was your way of protecting me, one last time. But my mind always circles back to the night before – that Saturday. 2nd March. The real beginning of the end.

***

I was out at a thirtieth birthday bash in a pub in Soho – definitely not my scene, but I had to show up for my old pal, Freddie. He'd hired a warm, oaky function room in a fancy pub, and invited me and Hugh – the Kings' School trio. Not sure if you remember, but we went to prom together, dateless, like the losers from *The Inbetweeners*.

My awkwardness hasn't changed. I felt awkward as hell at the party. I glued myself to Hugh, the only familiar face besides the birthday boy.

Around half-nine, I ended up outside the pub with Hugh and a few others, sipping lemonade and laughing at a ginger guy doing silly accents. They were terrible, but I was too people-shy to say mine were better. Then your name flashed on my phone, and confusion hit me. You never called this late.

'Everything ok?' Hugh noticed my frown.

'Yeah, should be. Sam's calling. I'll be back in a minute.'

I wandered to a quieter spot, where there were fewer tipsy folk, and answered – crossing my fingers for a casual goodnight.

You told me you weren't feeling well – something about your kidneys – and that Dad was racing you to Southampton General A&E, Mum and Megan waiting anxiously at 12 Sidders. I could hear the engine humming in the background.

'What? What happened?'

'It's ok, just not feeling that—that great. I'm sorry. Didn't want to worry you.'

I stared at the partygoers, frozen. Everyone else was still drinking and laughing. Ginger Guy still playing comedian. I felt numb.

'Shit, Sam⋯ I'll come home now. To help out.'

'No. No, you don't have to, Jack.' Your breaths were shallow, like you were struggling for air. 'You're in London. No point. I'll be fine.'

'Are you sure, Sam?'

'Yeah, honestly, it's—it's fine. Don't worry about it. I just wanted to let you know.'

I didn't want to accept it, but I had no choice. By the time I reached Waterloo, the platforms would've been empty. And I had no suitcase. It just wasn't going to happen. I was meant to stay in London with Agathe the night before you died. Your fate was in the hands of the doctors.

I checked my WhatsApp and saw an unread message from Dad, sent at 7:14 PM:

Yeh, about time Stoke won. Sam not very well. Really bad stomach cramps so had to come home & leave Megan in Soton, Mum gone to see show at Mayflower with her. Waiting now for ambulance, could be kidney stones but not sure.

Don't worry, will let you know once doctor has checked him over.

I didn't realise it was that bad, Sam. That you had to cut your Saturday with Megan short and head back to 12 Sidders. At least she still got to see the show. What show was it?

I guess Mum and Dad didn't want to worry me earlier in the day. Still – why hadn't I read that message sooner? I could've come home and been with you in A&E. Now it was nearly ten. I felt powerless.

I returned to the group, attempting a smile that fell flat.

'All ok?' Hugh asked.

'Sam's on his way to casualty.'

'What?'

'I'm sorry, man. I think I'm going to have to go.'

'Yeah, of course. Is he ok, though?'

'I hope so. Something about his kidneys.'

Hugh, being the true gent he is, walked me to Oxford Circus. Under the bright lights, he praised me for being a great brother, insisting there was nothing I could do – just like you told me over the phone. I nodded, pretended to agree. But once I descended into the station, the tears seeped out and drowned me all the way to Ealing Common.

I'm a bit of a tube-crier, aren't I, Sam?

I cried at home too, in front of Agathe. I felt so far away – imagining you waiting to be seen in the hospital while I lay in bed. I hoped you'd be alright, that it was just a minor hiccup. But kidney issues and Duchenne? Not a great combo. It could lead to complications. The thought of you possibly dying the next day didn't even cross my mind, though. I just felt bad for you, Mum, and Dad. It was like Christmas Eve all over again.

I called Dad: nothing.

I called Mum: nothing.

I called Megan: nothing.

I called you: nothing.

I texted Dad. I asked if you'd seen a doctor yet. He replied a few minutes later:

Sam being attended to now Jack. Hopefully home later this evening.

I replied, saying you'd be ok. That the two of you would be driving home soon. I'm not sure I believed it.

At 10:45 PM, another message came:

Not great Jack, stuck in a corridor in big queue waiting for a bay, Sam's on saline drip to keep him hydrated. Been standing for nearly 2hrs. No seats!

How was I supposed to sleep after that? I called you and Dad again. Still no answer. It must've been mayhem at Southampton General. As Agathe fell asleep, I lay in bed, restless – much like Mum and Megan at 12 Sidders. I kept refreshing my messages, and finally received this from Dad at midnight:

Still waiting to see doctors!

That's when I knew I had to call it a night. I was emotionally drained, and I didn't want to wake Agathe. I needed my energy for the morning. I'd contact you first thing, around half-six – your usually wake-up time, when the night splints came off. I'd call you and you'd tell me you were safe and sound in your bed. Your girlfriend asleep in my old room, Mum and Dad in theirs. Everything would be fine. A normal Sunday.

I never imagined that half-six would be the time you'd return to 12 Sidders.

You were discharged just before sunrise, around six. You and Dad pulled an all-nighter at A&E.

If I'd somehow reached you that Saturday night after Freddie's party, I probably would've watched you slip away the next day. Would that have broken me? Maybe. You knew I was fragile, Sam. Maybe your final smile – the one I saw Sunday night – was for me.

Jack, everything's fine. Look, I'm happy.

If that smile was meant for me, thank you. But I still wish I'd come home that Saturday night. I could've found a way – a taxi or a coach. Even if I'd arrived Sunday morning, at least I would've seen you. But you'd have said there was no point in me coming for the day, especially with work looming on Monday.

At half-six, I called you – just like I said I would. You'd just got home. You sounded exhausted but told me everything was ok, not knowing you'd die just twelve hours later. You just needed rest ahead of your scan on Monday. There was nothing I could do.

Anyway. I'm approaching the gates of a school that I've lost all enthusiasm for since you left. Usually, I write to you beyond the school gates, but not today. Too many kids around. And it's weird, writing about death while plastering on a smile for staff and students. They have no idea. It's quite funny. I could be plotting the demise of the school on my Word app, and they'd still greet me with grins.

Speak soon, Sam.

FRIDAY 10 MAY (EVENING)

Happy nine o'clock, Sam.

Just left Megan at Waterloo. Now I be heading home like she be doing.

We talked a lot, mostly about you and your Samness. She shared her excitement about her new school and her work with nurture groups and the SEND department, while I mentioned that I'm not thrilled to be back at Billy Bobs, but at least it keeps my mind off the heavy grief-sack I carry.

As I dipped chicken strips into sweet-spicy sauce, she dropped a bombshell that caught me off guard. You might already know – or maybe you don't – and perhaps that's for the best. Or maybe you'd actually welcome the news? Who the hell knows?

I'll just spill the Cannellinis. This Word document's my diary now. I'd be lying if I didn't lay bare what's weighing on my mind.

Megan has a new boyfriend – a former colleague. She says she's taking it slow, though she also has his photo on her screensaver. She's still mourning you, and he gets that. For me, it feels a little too soon – but that probably says more about where I am than where she is. Losing you was a real kick in the gut for her; she probably misses the companionship.

With your big heart, Samwise, I bet you'd find some comfort in knowing your eHarmony dream is getting on with her life instead of wallowing in sadness. Part of me struggles with it, but another part knows she deserves joy too.

Still, it feels strange. It feels like someone else has stepped in your place and stolen your girl – I still think of her as your girlfriend. I mean, she has your name inked on her arm. How am I supposed to see her differently?

What do I even call her now? She's not an ex; that suggests a breakup. I guess she's just Megan – Megan who's moving forward, holding someone's hand, yet still clutching onto memories of you.

She assured me you were her sole focus while you were an item. She thought of no one else – only you. I want you to know that, Sam. You were her world.

I feel envious of her in a way, of how she's able to move on and find a new boyfriend. I can't replace a brother. There's no healing that wound.

I'm on a Journey to See You, Sam is all I have. And once I stop typing, I'll truly be brotherless.

Maybe it's true that all we need are books and blank pages. They quietly listen and keep us connected.

A SUNNY SATURDAY

Well, well, well, Sammypops – new nickname alert. Lucky you!

I'm sitting on a park bench. Over yonder, there's a funfair that looks tacky as hell. There's this little ride that hoists you up, spins you around, then drops you back down. No. Thank. You. I hate those rides; they make my belly ache.

Funny, though··· it reminds me of your hoist at home. Yours spun and lifted you too, but gently, carefully – not like this aggressive fairground nonsense. Yours held you steady when the world around you couldn't.

But back to Ealing Common. And what a fitting name. Common chaos everywhere you look. Kids are screaming, kites flying in the too-blue sky, lanky guys wandering around with their hands in their pants, aggressive rap music blasting from their phones, and sassy girls with witchy-long nails snapping their best duck faces. It's all fun and games here. Park life!

Agathe's off gallivanting with her bestie from uni today, leaving me to my own devices. I've applied for three art teacher jobs and designed the Save the Date for the big do next year. It's been a productive morning, Samwells. The vampire's come out for some sunlight now.

There's a large, middle-aged man sprawled out on the grass in his swimming trunks and nothing else. His sunburnt skin looks like undercooked chicken. A family just walked past him, eyebrows raised··· and I'm boring myself documenting this.

I think that'll be all for today.

SUNDAY 12 MAY

Day six of this relentless heat, Samwells, and I'm too low to enjoy it. This morning, I woke up drenched in sweat, haunted by the impact your disability had on my life. It's moulded me through all the trials and tribulations. Douchebag Duchenne's meddled with my being.

Siblings often say they wouldn't be the person they are without their brother or sister. But for those of us with disabled siblings, that has a different level of truth to it.

The first scar Dooshy left on me was a suffocating sense of loneliness. Not that Mum and Dad neglected me or anything – they gave me a splendid childhood full of Beanie Babies and Shreddies. But you were always the focal point of our family, mollycoddled that little bit more. I learned early on that our family's mission was to keep you happy and healthy. Like you were a Tamagotchi pet – the sun in The Waddingtons' solar system.

I became an assistant parent at a premature age, sharing the load with The (actual) Parents. While other teens were busy being teens, fretting over trivial matters, I was preoccupied with you and the harsh realities of your condition. Your impending, horror-movie-style death. It was a heavy load for Jackyboy to carry. I envied those carefree children, unaware of how easy they had it – frolicking around with giggles and gossip, without the guilt of having fully functional legs. I looked at their innocent faces and thought: *you guys got no idea.*

But I never resented them. Nor did I resent you.

Yes, you drove me up the wall with your temper tantrums – like that time you thought spitting at me, Mum, or Dad when angry was a good idea, or when you marched up to that poor cashier at Thorpe Park to say you'd like to report your family to social services. Actually, looking back, that was pretty hilarious.

And I was jealous of your bond with Mum and Dad. I often felt on my ones. Like there was you three, and then there was me – diverting attention away from you. I was off learning to play the violin, going to art college, doing my tingaling, all the while feeling guilty for it.

I thought you deserved the spotlight, not me. My job was to take care of you, not chase my dreams. I was a looker-afterer with hidden talents, too ashamed to step into the light. What use was my creativity when my brother couldn't even pour a bowl of cereal for himself? It all felt so pointless – so indulgent.

My artistic flair felt like a curse: a dirty little secret I couldn't shake off. A stain that underlined how fortunate I was compared to you. That's why I preferred staying in my cramped bedroom, sketching tiny worlds in tiny sketchbooks – keeping my talent under wraps.

I had a few close friends growing up. So, I guess I wasn't always alone. I could be quite the social butterfly when the mood struck, enjoying the company of others. Teen Jack was too naïve to fully grasp the weight of sibling-shame, or the social anxiety that tagged along.

It simmered beneath the surface, but I kept the lid closed and forced myself to party like a normal teenager. Yet even with friends, I felt a profound disconnect. *Why am I out here talking, smiling, and sipping cider? I should be by my brother's side, feeling sad for him and his situation. What gives me the right to have fun?*

The second I caught myself feeling good around friends, paranoia punched me in the stomach.

You shouldn't be enjoying yourself, you heartless monster. What about your disabled brother? What about your sadness? That's what you should be feeling, you fool!

Fun meant potential anxiety, so I started socialising less.

I doubted my friends were bombarded with such self-loathing thoughts. They seemed to be living it up, and I envied them like crazy. I wished I could've just switched off the pain, but it was too embedded in me. I was spiralling into deeper depression and anxiety, developing a taste for melancholic music. Enter: The Cure, The Smiths, Sigur Rós. All that sad soppy shit I can't say goodbye to.

Over the years, I've traded social interaction for solitude, and now I'm the most socially awkward version of myself I've ever been. It worries me that I only have a handful of close chums. How am I meant to navigate life with so few?

Ok, that's enough. Time to cheer up. Agathe wants a hug. We're still in bed. She's craving some attention – and who can resist a good hug?

Hey, despite all this doom and gloom, at least I have a girlfriend, right?

WEDNESDAY 15 MAY

Morning, Sambosah.

I'm on the tube, bouncing along the rickety Piccadilly Line, heading to Billy Bobs. I've just wolfed down two croissants and a flat white – my go-to breakfast when I'm in a hurry. I snag them from the Tesco Express near the little flat I share with my sweet little dumpling, Agadoodoo.

I wanted to tell you about a gem of a video I watched while walking to Tesco. Remember those epic meltdown videos Mum used to film? She'd threaten to show them to your friends to expose your inner monster. Well, I found one on her phone a few weeks back when she let me transfer photos of you over to mine – I think she forgot she still had this little treasure. It's the only one she kept. Usually, she deleted them after you calmed down. They were empty threats, really – just cheeky tactics to try and curb your tantrums. Samtrums. Which, let's be honest, never really worked. Not a lot stopped you, Sammyboys. You were a force to be reckoned with. Linda called you the Ayatollah once. So true.

I've had that mighty video on loop since uploading it. Dad's trying to calm you down because you're about to launch a bowl across the conservatory. Standard. You were riled up for whatever reason, like the girl from *The Exorcist.* Dad's leaning over you, telling you to control yourself. Mum's filming and threatening to show your friends the *real, demonic you.* And I'm sitting at the dining table, advising you to take it easy.

Feeling cornered, you felt the need to shout, 'Fuck off, you cunts!' at one point. You were a loose cannon that evening.

Watching the video back made me laugh at first. Your small, furious face cursing on camera had me in stitches. But then it morphed into second-hand embarrassment. The way your eyes drooped after those four hurtful words showed just how drained and ashamed you were. I doubt you meant to unleash it on us – the frustration just got the better of you, didn't it?

I doubt all those meds helped either. Granny always said it was understandable you lost your cool when things didn't go your way. Believe me, if I were in your chair, I'd be hurling objects and cursing more than I already do.

Sure, you had your devilish moments. I had to walk on eggshells around you – watch what words came out of my mouth, and how I delivered them. Avoiding words you despised, like *yep* and *please*, became an art form. And I had to watch the way I looked at you, knowing you hated *judgemental eyes*. If I slipped up, you'd erupt and fire questions at me like a prosecutor:

Why did you say that?

Were you trying to annoy me?

You don't even care what I'm speaking about, do you?

It's rude to say yep, *you know?*

If I failed to provide the right explanation – and I rarely could – you'd retreat to your lair, close the door, and dissect the incident like a crime scene. I wish I could dig up those reports you etched in your notebooks. Maybe you disposed of them as you grew up, not wanting to relive those days.

But allow me to resurrect one – an imaginary report, if you will.

From Sam Waddington, the Notetaker General:

I didn't like the way Jack replied to my comment about the football game. It was unacceptable. He said yep *to me when he knows I don't like it when people say that word. It implies they're not listening to what I'm saying, like they don't care, and this doesn't feel nice. It's actually quite cruel. My family should know better.*

But Jack might have said yep *because he was focused on the football match and not what I was saying, so he just said* yep *to give the impression he was listening. This is a normal thing people do when they're concentrating on something else. They don't give their full attention to the other person talking. This is probably what happened when Jack said* yep.

People will say yep *in my life. Family, carers, friends. I think I just have to accept that this word will keep popping up, even if it pisses me off.*

Wow. I'm quite proud of what I've written there, Sam. My memory serves me well.

I remember asking you to share your reports after you'd calmed down and taken the lift downstairs. You were hesitant, but eventually relented. I'd read them and laugh at how you bitched about me in your tiny Moleskine. You'd end up sniggering too. You knew it was ridiculous, but it was something you needed to do. It helped you process things.

Sometimes, Mum and I would deliberately use *yep* to wind you up and try to desensitise you to this specific way of saying *yes*.

'Yep yep yep yep yep. Yep yep yep yep yep,' we'd laugh.

It drove you nuts. We were careful, though – if you became too agitated, we'd back off. We didn't want you throwing things or spitting at us. You had a deadly aim when your arms were stronger. I still remember the time you tossed a knife at me, Sam. Not too sharp, thank God. Missed my eye, left a small bruise on my forehead.

Bloody wild.

Anyway. My year elevens will be piling into my classroom in fifteen minutes. We're paper weaving sepia and black-and-white portraits in the style of Greg Sand. Their coursework theme's *Distortion in Portraiture.* Mr. Sand's one of my go-to artists for this project – easy to replicate, effective, great for the lower-ability kids. Google him if you've got··· wait for it··· Sky-Fi!

Sorry.

THURSDAY 16 MAY

Sam, I need a wee breather. A tactical break. Reason being I've got an interview at a posh girls' school next week. I'm trying to start a new chapter, add a bit of sparkle to this dreary existence – just like you would've wanted.

Peace out, bedrin – I've been listening to a lot of reggae these days, Sam. A likkle bit of Gregory Isaacs, a likkle bit of Freddie McGregor. One love, Brother.

LIFE ADMIN

MONDAY 20 MAY

I got three options, Sam Boy. None feel right.

Option one: stick with Billy Bobs. It has its moments, but the pay's good, it's local, and I could cycle in. Tubes are expensive. Maybe save some doh with an e-bike, shave the commute down.

Option two: jump ship to the fancy girls' school in Kingston – if I get the offer. Better school, worse pay, longer commute. Citymapper says forty-six-minutes by bike.

Option three: take the Kingston job and move nearby. No commute. Leafy riverside walks. A fresh start.

But Agathe's rooted to London. Kingston feels like exile to her. She's already compromised a lot.

She stuck by me when I left her in London and moved to Portsmouth after lockdown to be closer to you. I was lonely there. She was lonely in London. But we made it work: weekend trains, long phone calls. Others might've called it quits. Long-distance relationship? Brother over lover? But The Agatron stayed. I owe her for that.

So, for now, I'll hold off Kingston.

Option one's the simplest: no move, no readjusting. I can survive Billy Bobs another year. If it all goes tits up come September, I'll job-hunt again. Schools are always scrounging for staff, aren't they?

You'd probably tell me to take the easy route: *Brother Jack, you've been through enough. You might even learn to love Billy Bobs. Get an e-bike and give yourself a break!'*

***

Screw it, Sam. I'll try option two.

Sorry, but I had to boot another kid out of class today. Billy Bobs is wearing me down. Behaviour there is beastly – like Eastleigh. I've worked in better schools – like the Catholic one in Portsmouth, where the kids were calmer and the rules were stricter. I can do it again.

Forty-five minutes to Kingston from our flat. With an e-bike? You're having a laugh, Citymapper. I reckon I could nail it in thirty. I'll test it tonight. The interview's tomorrow. If it goes well, I might just go for it, Sam.

Now, where's a Lime bike when you need one?

TUESDAY 21 MAY

Interview day, Sam.

The trek from my flat to the fancy girls' school is a hellish ordeal – without the e-bike, that is. Quickest I managed with the aid of public transport: fifty minutes. Two tubes and a bus. I know it won't be every day, since cycling will be the norm – last night's bike trial only took, wait for it, thirty blooming minutes (told you, Citymapper!) – but still.

Also, what about during the winter? When it's too cold to cycle, or when it's tipping it down? I'd have to wake up at stupid o'clock for a bitchy commute, then get back late. Doesn't sound appealing.

Not sure what to do, Sambobs. I could really do with one of your phone calls right now.

You'd tell me to chill, wouldn't you? First things first. See if you even get the job before stressing over the nitty-gritty.

WEDNESDAY 22 MAY

The school was amazing, Sam. Holy guacamole. If I get the job, I'll lose my marbles.

I've been glued to my inbox all day, hammering refresh every two minutes during my breaks. The headteacher swore he'd let me know today. Now it's ten past four. I've heard nothing.

The tension is torturous. I have this sickly feeling in my stomach – a feeling of unknowing. I'm stuck in limbo and it's horrible. One phone call determines whether I'm destined for a posh palace of learning… or another year in the dungeon of despair. (Kidding – I love you really, Billy Bobs. Kind of.)

THURSDAY 23 MAY

Well, after all of that, Sam⋯ I didn't get it.

Oh well. Shit happens. Like your death.

Guess I'm staying at Billy Bobs for another year. At least I won't have to worry about adjusting to a new school – no putting on brave faces in front of unfamiliar ones, no pretending life's all fine and dandy. And hey, the current school pays better. That comforts me. Money matters, Samwells. I can take it easy now. No more life admin.

***

I'm a good brother.

I keep telling myself that. Fiona the talking therapist thinks it's a smart idea.

I often wonder if I really am – you know, a good brother. Especially after you broke your leg twice in my company. Sure, they were jaccidents, but they still haunt me. You texted me from the ward that night saying you were lucky to have me as your bro, but I didn't believe you. I felt like a big piece of shit, leaving you alone in hospital over Christmas.

Now, looking back, I see you were right. I am a good brother.

Am I even a brother anymore, though? Or have I morphed into an only child?

Christ.

***

Just Googled: *How to have a wedding when you're an introvert.*

It's happening this time next year, Sam. The Agatron and Jacko, tying the knot. I've sent out my Save the Dates. I designed them in my fineliner style – spiky font, floral border. Seventy people have confirmed already. Seventy! My stomach's doing flips.

I hate having a crowd staring at me and all my angles. Speeches. First dance. Bloody hell. Public speaking was my personal horror show growing up. Standing up and presenting in class? Instant panic attacks.

Did I ever tell you how I used to get embarrassed by the right side of my face? Probably didn't. I didn't tell anyone. Definitely some undiagnosed facial dysmorphia there. I should've mentioned it to someone when I was younger – how I thought the right side of my face was disturbing and ugly, how my jaw looked like it belonged to a donkey, how my eyes were all wonky from the Bell's palsy, how my hair sat awkwardly on my head.

Every morning I'd check the mirror and hope I didn't look like a freakazoid. It never worked. I'd leave the house feeling ashamed of the hideous right side – like I was the Elephant Man. Nuts, isn't it? Especially considering I thought the left side of my face was pretty decent. Polar opposites.

It's not so bad now. I show the right side of my face every day – it's out there in the open. I'm less embarrassed than I was in my teens and early twenties. That feels like progress.

But enough about the right side of my face.

The wedding speech is a whole new level of dread. All those silent eyes on me, waiting for my words to tumble out. My trembling voice and nervous gulps. The collective cringe as the audience hope I don't turn tomato-red and bolt for the nearest exit.

Once, in college, I made a break for the bathroom mid-English lesson, hoping the teacher would forget I existed. Spoiler: she didn't. I had to stand up and ramble about baby babbling or something – I baby-babbled through the whole thing. My ears were glowing, my voice like a frightened toddler's.

It's a miracle I can teach at all.

As for the wedding speech – I'll manage. But it's hard to feel any excitement knowing my best man won't be there.

Much to Agathe's irritation – she's turning into a bit of a bridezilla lately. No offence, Agathe, but it's literally all that's on your mind. A bit like how my godly brother's all that's on mine.

I felt safer with you around, Sam. You were my shield. I hid behind you like a cowardly knight.

The carer brother – that was my role. Or maybe yours?

I felt bound to you. And now··· I'm lost trying to do Jack without you.

You were the best part of me. I mean that.

What's my role now?

<hr>

Y O U

MONDAY 3 JUNE

Hello, my dear little brother, Sammyboy Jeffries.

You've been on my mind all day – like a first crush. I couldn't stop picturing you: sun-kissed skin, piercing eyes, your thick, bushy eyebrows. Scrumdiddlyumptious. Your cheeky round face and that mop of dark brown hair came together like a portrait by an old master – a Rembrandt, let's say.

Your glowing face, thin lips, and all that curly chaos kept intruding at the most inconvenient moments: while I was demonstrating oil painting techniques to my year nines, or glugging water between lessons. Every time, my heart sank.

Not now, Sam.

It's 10:22 PM. I'm in bed. My phone screen's pulling my eyes open, even with the brightness turned down. I thought I'd write to you – well, to clear you from my mind, quite frankly. You know how songs get stuck in your head, and the only way to forget them is to listen again? That's my plan. So, here's me, squeezing in a message before I visit Beddybyeland.

I want to tell you how great you were – how funny – like the time you drunkenly serenaded us in that pub in the New Forest. You ready?

***

We'd just polished off our Sunday roasts – Jacko, Samo, The Parents, and The Frenchy – and while we browsed the dessert menus, you vanished. Off to the bar.

You weren't fussed about pudding. What you craved was more booze. A pint of Guinness, to be exact. You already had a Sex on the Beach swirling around your system, and the countryside brightness had lit you up.

I watched you manoeuvre your chair with wobbly grace and a mischievous grin. You knew what you were doing. And you knew your big brother was watching, ready to cackle.

Mum warned me: 'Don't give him the attention, Jack. He's only getting another drink to show off. You know what he's like.'

'Yeah, I know,' I replied. But I looked anyway.

Each time our eyes locked, we shared giggles like two misbehaving children in a classroom. You parked your chair in a little corner of the bar, bent your head down toward the glass, because you couldn't lift it up, and sipped your bitter drink like it was some dark, sacred ritual. I lost it.

Agathe frowned beside me. Bless her. I don't think she wanted to see drunk Sam. Sober Sam was already something.

I think you retreated to the corner of that bar out of sheer embarrassment, unable to face us while you nursed your pint – better to indulge in your shameful business alone. You also wouldn't have been able to carry your pint back to the table. You looked like one of those unfortunate men you see at Wetherspoons during the middle of the day. Comedy gold – an image lodged into my mind for years to come.

You raised your glass and downed the dregs like a champ, flashing a grin at the bartender before strutting back to the table, pride oozing from every pore.

Look at me. I can order a drink at a bar on my own. I can get drunk if I choose to.

A young waiter approached to take our dessert orders – except yours.

'I'm good on dessert, thanks. I've had a lot to drink. But I'll take another Sex on the Beach, please, Sir.'

The look on the waiter's face was priceless. He didn't see that coming.

But I did. That familiar glint in your eye told me you were ready to steal the show again. You knew everyone was trying to ignore your drunkenness, so you devised a way to get back in the spotlight. It worked. We all laughed – the waiter included, though he hesitated, unsure if it was ok to chuckle at someone in a wheelchair. Just the way it goes sometimes.

While we waited for our sweet treats, you said you needed the toilet. Jackpot! I couldn't wait to say yes; escorting my drunk brother to the disabled loo sounded like an absolute blast.

It was a workout. You were a floppy mess, and it took ages for you to go about your business. And you wouldn't stop talking, rambling on about anything.

'I've made a fool out of myself, haven't I, Brother Jack?'

'Because you drank a Guinness on your own?'

'Yeah··· whoopsy.'

I noticed you were holding your URIsack loosely, not really paying attention to all the urine gushing out of you. I gestured toward the accident waiting to happen.

'Careful, Sam.'

'Oh crap.'

We laughed. I emptied your dark-yellow pee, handed you wet wipes.

'You should drink some water. Pee's a bit yellow.'

'Shit. Ok. Can you get me a glass of water when we're back?'

'Sure thing, scallywagle.'

You snorted. '*Scallywagle*. You're a funny brother, Jack. I hope I've not embarrassed you in front of Agathe.'

'Of course you haven't. She's been drunk before. And she's seen you drunk before.'

'I feel like every time I see her, I'm drunk or tipsy. She doesn't see me sober anymore.'

I snorted this time. 'That's because she usually sees you when we go out for a meal, or on a special occasion, like a birthday. It's fine, Sam. She's seen you sober plenty of times too. It's just that now, you're a raging alcoholic.'

'Hey! I'm embarrassed now. I bet she actually thinks I'm an alcoholic.'

'Probably.'

'Really?'

'Of course not.'

You caught a glimpse of your blurred reflection in the mirror. 'It's humiliating being this drunk.'

'Well, yeah. When you're drunk, you can do silly things. It can be very humiliating.'

'Is that why you're a teetotaller?'

'Maybe. To save myself the shame. But I get embarrassed even when I'm sober. Look, you're absolutely fine. Agathe finds it funny.'

'Does she?'

'Yeah.' I put your wet wipes in the bin while you fastened your Velcro jogging bottoms and shuffled back into your chair. 'We all do. It's nice seeing you let loose. You never got to go out and get drunk in your teens like I did. You're making up for lost time. Just maybe have less in the future. You don't need to push your limits. You'll feel better if you stay within them.'

'But I don't know my limits. I shouldn't have had that Guinness. Silly Sam.'

'Well, now you have a better idea. Now you know not to have a Guinness straight after two sexy beaches.'

'True⋯' You turned on your chair – the beautiful beeps I'll sorely miss.

'I'm a sexy beach, aren't I?'

'Yes. You're a sexy beach.'

'Ok, time to go back out. I need to act sober. I feel like I might be sick.'

'Drink some water. It'll help.'

You nodded. 'I'll definitely do that, Brother Jack. What a kind, older sibling I have.'

After our little bathroom banter, we rejoined the group and, to everyone's surprise, you zoomed straight to Agathe and mumbled an apology for being intoxicated. She accepted it and told you not to worry.

But on the drive home, you were at it again. You barked at Mum to plug in your phone, demanded 'Sexbomb,' and sang along like a sloppy drunk – eyes closed, face contorted, hips shuffling back and forth.

You gave it your all, Sam. It was chaos. Sheer brilliance.

Agathe was flummoxed. She'd seen you tipsy before, but never enough to gyrate to 'Sexbomb' – maybe this should've been the closing song at your funeral party after all. I told her you did this even sober – just with a little less flair.

Watching you perform was always a riot. I wish I could revisit your Michael Jackson impersonation at the Kings' School concert, pre-wheelchair. Your legs were Duchenne legs – tip-toed and not the most reliable – but somehow, they made your shimmy and moonwalk even more impressive. You couldn't walk properly, but you could shamone across the floor like the King of Pop himself, as if those tricky little tiptoe legs had a secret rhythm of their own. I don't know many twelve-year-olds who'd don a sequinned glove and shamone to the music in front of an audience. You had some guts, saMJ.

But look. I loved you drinking and enjoying getting drunk. You never got drunk in your teens like I did – going out to house parties and clubs and festivals, not knowing your limits, making regretful decisions. You never experienced any of that. This was your reckless phase. In your mid-twenties. You were still young. Why shouldn't you enjoy it?

Anyway. I should hit the hay. Train to Beddybyeland's arriving in five.

***

Just brushed me teeth. One last thing before Beddybyeland:

SPECTRUM's planning an event in your honour. I spotted the poster on Facebook. One of your co-workers has asked me to compile a playlist and some photos. It's beautiful. But it also feels like I'm preparing for your second funeral.

***

Seriously, last one now. It's nearly midnight and I've got school tomorrow.

You always had to look up at people. Not metaphorically. Literally. In your chair, surrounded by standing figures. I wonder how that felt⋯ Did you ever think about it?

I hated how Douchebag Duchenne squashed you short. You were much taller than five foot three. Maybe that's why you loved dogs so much – something to look down on. Something to care for.

Am I onto something? Or am I just chatting a load of old codswallop?

WEDNESDAY 5 JUNE

Morning, Sam.

I feel like reminiscing for a couple of days. I'm too tired to write about anything new. New means without you. And that's hard to do.

Let's kick things off with my hardback copy of *Rebecca* by Daphne du Maurier. Remember the one? And how you decided to deface it? You vicious vandal.

With a bold blue biro, you transformed the yellowed inside cover into a masterpiece of immaturity – a cartoon penis surrounded by the words *POO, BUM, TITS, BALLS,* and *WILLY,* all in glorious capital letters. You were about eighteen at the time of the crime. You did it because you knew how much I loved that battered old book – and you wanted to piss me off. Probably because I said *yep.* And it worked.

Your drawing did piss me off. But it also made me laugh. I was in a giggling fit for days.

The sheer absurdity of it. How crudely you'd drawn the penis – with six spiky lines poking out from each testicle to mimic pubic hair. A true work of art. Something out of a David Shrigley drawing.

I found that book in a charity shop in Beastly Eastleigh years ago, just like many of my other worn treasures. I've always enjoyed unearthing forgotten scraps within books – scribbled notes, faded postcards, abandoned bookmarks.

But nothing quite prepared me for finding a hand-drawn penis on the first page of *Rebecca.*

I sometimes imagine someone else picking up that same book in a charity shop – if I'd donated it after your little artistic endeavour – and their face when they opened to page one: your blue biro scrawl of profanity and penis.

How funny would that be?

But I can't part with Becky de Winter. She's a keeper. A cherished relic. All thanks to that small, spiky dick you drew inside her.

THURSDAY 6 JUNE 2024

Memory number two coming your way, Sam.

Remember the time you bought a random bonsai tree online? You got all starry-eyed about it, treating it like a new pet. The pug you never had. You said that buying the little green orb felt like you were giving birth. I didn't realise you had experience with childbirth, Sam?

That fuzzy ball of foliage needed to be soaked in water every now and then, which I thought was totally bizarre. Forgetting to order a stand, you placed it in a cereal bowl Mum lent you. You named him Bertie the Bonsai. You even bought it a little buddy in the form of a Buddha figurine, as well as a plaque with *Bertie* engraved on it. That made me bellow.

'Plaques are for the dead, Sam.'

'I know. I got it as a joke.'

'Do you foresee it dying soon?'

'No. I'll look after him.'

But I could see the worry creeping into your eyes. Our family had a notorious track record with pets – I raise my cup of cardamom tea (I bloody love cardamom tea now, Sam, by the way) to that poor old gerbil who met his end under your lift. We found him a week after he escaped from its cage, looking like a cartoon character who'd been squished flat.

'At least you have a plaque, Sam. We could always bury Bertie in the garden and put the plaque on top of his grave when the time comes.'

'Ha ha ha. Very funny. Maybe.'

Before Bertie finally succumbed to the inevitable – two months after you gave birth to him (who knew a bonsai tree could be so difficult to raise?) – he became the centrepiece of your makeshift bonsai shrine on your chest of drawers. Bertie was living the high life with Buddha, his plaque, a handful of blue pebbles, pruning scissors, and a fertiliser-and-water spray bottle. Quite the crew.

Mum and I teased you about it, like we did with most of your projects. As Bertie's health declined and he turned a parched yellow, Mum would refer to him as a *dried-up bollock of a bonsai*. She had a wicked sense of humour, didn't she? But it was peculiar how Bertie sprouted from this singular, hairy moss ball. It looked like something out of a David Cronenberg film.

You kept babysitting the little green creature right until his final moments, dousing his large bollock with fertiliser-and-water solution. Snipping away at his wilting leaves with your tiny scissors, watching them drop off like it was constantly autumn. Bertie was balding. Embarrassed by his lack of head hair, he finally let go and called it quits. That once vibrant green bollock turned a sad shade of yellow. Bertie was history.

Instead of giving him a proper send-off, like I thought you might, you tossed the dried-up bollock of a bonsai in the compost bin.

Bye bye, Bertie.

I miss Bertie.

FRIDAY 7 JUNE

I discovered something today, Sam, while rummaging through one of your diaries in the open cabinet by the living room door. I was on a little treasure hunt, searching for traces of your large, confident handwriting – to bring you back to life for a short while. That's what I do these days. I try to summon you with paper and ink. Like you a jinn.

You had three diaries. What I found was tucked inside the one from 2021: three A4 pages, stapled in the top left corner, folded like they were trying to hide. They practically yelled, *Don't read me!* So, of course, Brother Big Nose did.

It was a doctor's letter. Marked Private and Confidential. Paragraphs galore, bold subheadings, a large, wavy signature at the bottom. I felt wrong for peeking, but curiosity got the better of me.

I was hoping to find out if you'd mentioned me to your GP. Was I part of the reason you spiralled into that dark pit? I needed to know if I was the villain in your story, for my own peace of mind. I wanted my conscience clear. So Brother Big Nose stuffed the doctor's report into his suitcase and went about his day, lips zipped.

Now here I am on a warm Friday evening, wondering if I'm about to cross the line. But shouldn't we be able to talk about these things? Depression shouldn't be a dirty little secret, right?

Growing up, I thought mine would just pack its bags and leave – a phase, temporary teenage angst. I tried to toughen up, thinking I'd simply outgrow it. And now I'm thirty, and it's still here – whispering my name, urging me to surrender.

You're not fit for this world, Jacko.

I wish I'd asked for help sooner. I thought strength meant silence. But ignoring those feelings only lets them fester – until you just can't take it any longer.

I know DMD did that to you. It wasn't just your body it tore into – it messed with your head as well. And those steroids, the ones you needed to stop your muscles turning to mush, didn't exactly make things easier. They kept you going, but they also wound you tight.

I've been clutching these three stapled A4 sheets since I stumbled upon them, tucking them into my fresh copy of *What's Eating Gilbert Grape* so Mum and Dad wouldn't see what I'd found. The book's not as good as the film – Johnny and Leo smashed that one – but it still hit close to home. I always thought of Gilbert and Arnie as The Waddington Brothers. Maybe that's why I keep your letter hidden inside those pages, holding Arnie's story and yours together.

I know I shouldn't have read it, Sam. But keeping it to myself felt even worse. This information shouldn't stay alone with me. Should I have thrown it away? I don't know. Maybe you can help.

I knew you were down in the dumps at times, and I knew it had a lot to do with your disability. But that wasn't enough for me. I wanted to get to the marrow. I wanted to know if I had a part to play. I craved your real feelings – what you didn't tell me, Mum, and Dad. You didn't go into too much detail when you were alive. Even to me, your go-to confidant, who you told everything to.

Yes, you mentioned how hard it was being disabled and single, but I wanted to unravel more layers. I thought this report might shed some light.

It brought me back to that impossible waiting list – the one you were stuck on during Covid. The NHS was overwhelmed. You reached out for help, and they pushed you away. They said unless you were feeling suicidal, they wouldn't take your request for medication and counselling any further. How ignorant and inhumane – denying support to someone with a physical disability. Mental health issues come with physical disabilities; it's part of the package. How could they not see that?

You in your chair, struggling to keep up with the rest of the world, was surely enough to prove you might be suffering from depression. That really did grind my gears, Samwise: the way they brushed you aside.

They didn't take your sadness seriously because you didn't explicitly mention suicidal thoughts, even though you'd felt that way at times. But you chose not to mention it. Perhaps out of embarrassment, or was it denial? Whatever the reason, it didn't matter. They had no business ignoring your SOS like that.

You were clearly wrestling with misery in your early-to-mid-twenties, often getting all teary-eyed while I was caring for you. It was eating up my insides seeing you like that, and I just couldn't witness it anymore. I urged you to do whatever it took to get on that waiting list, because you were a fighter, just like me. Just like Mum and Dad. Just like every other family batting Douchebag Duchenne.

'Tell them what they want to hear, Sam,' I said one evening while drying you off with your *Jaws* towel after your shower. 'Tick their stupid box. Say you're feeling suicidal.'

You wiped a tear away. 'Ok. I will.'

'It's not a lie, right? You told me how you wanted to end it all. You said it because you wanted help. I doubt you ever meant to go through with it, but those thoughts were as real as my bad jokes.'

'Yeah, they were real.'

'Exactly!'

I closed the bathroom door, conscious I might have been speaking a bit too loud – too passionately. This was a brother-to-brother conversation, not a family meeting. I didn't want to worry The Parents after their busy days at work.

After ruffling your damp, curly hair, I pulled you in for a big hug. 'It's all going to be alright, Sam.'

'Thanks. I hope so. And it's true, I did have those thoughts. I should probably tell the doctors. I should be honest with them.'

'You should, Sam. That's how you'll get the help you need. Simples.' Then I clicked my tongue like that grating meerkat from the Compare the Market ads.

Your eyes were puffy, cheeks sticky with tears, but you managed a smile. 'Sorry for crying like this in front of you. I don't want you to worry.'

'I'm so glad you're opening up. I can't imagine how tough it is living with a disability. I really can't. There's only so much I can say. And I don't want to say the wrong thing. I'm a depressive. I probably can't offer the best advice. You need to speak to professionals.'

'Ok. I will. I want to get better.'

Before opening the door and rolling you into your bedroom – one of my favourite places in the world – I gave you another squeeze. 'You're the bravest person I know, Sam.'

The next day, you took my brotherly advice and reached out to the NHS again, telling them how it was. How it actually was. You dropped the S word and made it clear you needed to be seen ASAP. You said you needed to get on that waiting list, and it paid off. They threw some citalopram your way, then set you up with counselling. I'm no chemist, and you didn't talk much about it, but I assume the effects of the pills were subtler and took a while to get into your system? But the therapy? That was your rocket fuel. You soaked up the therapist's advice like Bertie's bollock soaking up water. You focused on the positives, kept a thought diary, bought self-help books, and made sure to do things that brought you joy. You practically forced happiness upon yourself. I was bursting with pride for my little bro, but I won't lie, a twinge of envy crept in too.

I never pushed myself to get better like you did. I just let myself drown in sadness, struggling to find a way out. But I'm making an effort now. I'm taking a leaf from your book. I'm having counselling, popping antidepressants with my morning coffee, and trying to see the sunnier side of life. I'm giving it a good go. After over twenty years of feeling blue, I'm not keen on spending another twenty in the same boat.

The report detailed your little research into obtaining a firearm. You opened up to me about those dark moments when you contemplated checking out early, and I shared my own experiences with those thoughts. But I had no clue about your sneaky little Google. The doc said you only looked into it once. After ten minutes of browsing, you realised how ridiculous it was. Thank goodness for that, Sammy.

I've definitely searched for ways out too, but deep down I knew I'd never follow through. I was just acting on impulse and curiosity. I imagine that's how it was for you as well. You considered it, but it was a fleeting thought. Bringing up the firearm was the game changer, though. Once a patient mentions a plan of action, doctors take it seriously. It was a smart move telling them. You played their games well.

I scanned the report some more, searching for my name or the word *brother*. I found it near the end, where you spoke about your family. You described me as *supportive* and *very honest with you*, which sometimes *upset* you, but you appreciated the *openness* since not many were that way with you. It was a bittersweet read, knowing my honesty might've caused you some distress.

I remember when I encouraged you to move out for your independence and to give Mum and Dad a break. Did that make you feel like a burden? If so, I'm sorry. You'd expressed wanting to move out of 12 Sidders eventually. I thought a little bruv-nudge was in order, just like you did for me when I needed it.

You told the doc that my honesty helped you *maintain your independence where you could*. He noted you spoke *warmly* about me, which made me smile. I'm glad you were fond of me, Sam. I've always thought the world of you. Sometimes I overshared because I believed that's what you wanted. I didn't want to pussyfoot around you. You wanted to be treated like everyone else, and I always spoke to you with good intentions.

I wasn't the cause of your depression, and neither were The Parents. Or you, for that matter. It was Douchebag Duchenne. Sure, maybe you'd have been down in the dumps even without the disease, but it defo played a starring role.

You lived with your depression for a while, bathed in it, gave into it, but eventually you told it to fuck off.

Got to try harder than that, Dooshy.

You shoved it aside like you did with all the other shit life threw at you.

You wanted the same opportunities as those who didn't have to deal with disabilities. You said it was tough to accept that your body couldn't always do what others took for granted. You longed for a relationship, or at least some kind of intimacy, and the fact you hadn't had that by the time of your referral three years ago likely triggered your funk and frustration. You wanted your own space, your own keys, and the responsibility of paying your own bills. You wanted to feel more self-assured. You wanted to avoid taking out your frustrations out on Mum, Dad, or me in the form of anger outbursts – throwing or smashing things. You didn't want to act out by throwing yourself off the bed when you were upset, forcing your family to bear the brunt of your moods. You said you didn't expect therapy and meds to completely cure your low mood or anxiety, but you hoped they'd help you handle your emotions.

And they did just that, Sam. They didn't cure you – but they helped you hold on. You never did move out of 12 Sidders, but you gave it a good shot. Last year, you chucked your name in the hat for the housing waiting list with Hampshire Homechoice – goddamn waiting lists! – and sent them a letter from your GP and neuromuscular nurse up in London, proving your need for live-in carers to *enjoy life with family and friends*. Yes, Big Nose peeked at the email the other day; I figured you wouldn't mind.

Honestly, though, knowing you were staring down the barrel of death this year, I wouldn't have wanted you to be away from your family in a little accessible flat. That would've been a real bummer. Probably for the best you spent your final moments at 12 Sidders with Mum and Dad – and me when I visited my old digs. We were able to hold on to you just a little longer.

SUNDAY 16 JUNE

June! Bloody June, Sam. It's pouring outside, and here I am, bundled up in my winter coat. This isn't summer; it's a pathetic excuse for it. Not impressed. Bring on Singys and Indys — just fifty-nine more sleeps.

You were thrilled for me and my first Southeast Asian adventure. You always wanted to see the world — to feel it, breathe it, and get lost in it — but it wasn't easy for you. So instead, you lived it through others. You'd track my flight paths on your phone, not missing a beat. I wish I could sneak you onto the plane with me.

In a way, I will be — because Teddy's coming with me. Just now, I've decided. He's basically you, right? Like a voodoo doll. I'll pack him — you — in my backpack and pull him — you — out every now and then to show him — you — the sights. He — you — will be my Saint Christopher, guiding me on my journey. Agathe will roll her eyes, but she's got her own quirks — she sniffs her doudou every night before bed. Doudou's French for teddy.

I realise I haven't written to you in over a week. My bad. What have I been up to? Not much, really. A lot of what Fiona calls *restorative practice*. Everyday things — work and keeping busy. Mundane activities that stop me from dwelling on my loss.

You'll be pleased to know I've been putting my foot down at work. Not letting myself be micromanaged or shushed. I'm here for the long haul, Sam, so I demanded full autonomy over a project I was excited about — revamping part of the year nine curriculum. A twelve-lesson printmaking project.

Once I started planning and sharing my tried-and-tested ideas from previous schools, the powers above at Billy Bobs snubbed them without any valid reasoning. What stung was that I pitched not one, but three solid ideas – all stronger than what's currently being taught. It felt like a kick in the gut.

So I stopped throwing out new ideas just to be shot down. Instead, I held my ground, defended my proposals, and reminded them they were fully in line with the curriculum goals. After much persistence, I finally got the green light to pimp out the projects my way. I felt a real rush of pride – standing up for myself, refusing to be dismissed. Dignity intact.

Building up my confidence, Sam.

Well done, Brother Jack.

On another note, I'm totally glued to this show called *The Walking Dead*. There's something oddly soothing about watching zombies get their gooey heads chopped off. People dropping like flies, characters drowning in grief – it's a reminder that my life isn't nearly as bleak as theirs. I'm doing ok in comparison.

I'm concentrating on living, Sam – just like you did. It's tough, but I'm making it work.

I crashed at 12 Sidders last night and now I'm back in London, riding the tube. Mum and Dad were ok. Not great, but ok. Mum only broke down twice. She's your biggest fan, Sam. Dad didn't cry – he rarely does these days. He's so adaptable, though I suspect he's bottling up a lot. Remarkably, I didn't cry either. The three of us Waddingtons did pretty well.

We had a pub lunch in Otterbourne, then I watched a few football games with Dad while Mum busied herself in her art room, making ginkgo leaf prints. After the football, I showed her how to cut out and paper-weave some of her prints into a checkerboard pattern like Mr. Sand. She liked the process and said she'd keep at it once I'm back in London. It's good to see her making art again. It lifts her spirits.

What else is new? The Parents are buying a bench for you – to sit in the churchyard across from 12 Sidders. They spoke to the vicar, and he's been helping them with the logistics. You'll be clamped down under a big oak tree, facing the stained-glass windows of the church. Lovely jubbly. Just hoping the birds don't shit on you.

We finalised the plaque wording this morning:

SAM WADDINGTON'S BENCH
1997-2024
We love you and will never forget you

Mum's ordering the plaque next week. We went with all caps for the first line to honour your love of capital letters. I think it's a beautiful idea – a place for people to sit and remember you. And a bench feels fitting since you spent so much of your life bum-bound.

I'm still sad most of the time. And angry. Sometimes, I get this wild urge to smash something – not to hurt anyone, just to kick and punch and throw things. Inanimate things. But it's hard to do it with people always around. I've thought about exercising, but it doesn't give me the release I'm after. I need to create some damage. Ignoring this itch is becoming increasingly difficult.

I know that if I returned to meditation, I could observe these thoughts and sensations and let them pass without reacting. But focusing on the impermanence of my thoughts and bodily sensations isn't part of my routine right now. I just want to find a good spot to toss a plate – like an abandoned carpark – and watch it shatter into a million pieces.

Maybe I'll try it. Or maybe I won't. You'd probably cheer me on either way.

Still, I don't think I'm badass enough for that kind of full-blown anti-social behaviour. Plus, I really should keep working on my anger management.

I've made progress since the time I launched a bottle of sunflower oil across the flat last October. Not my finest hour. I never told you about it – kept that one quiet.

Agathe witnessed the oily outburst. The bottle missed her by a few feet and exploded on the floor – oil everywhere, seeping into the cracks between the floorboards. Cleaning it was hell; I went through half a bottle of disinfectant. Ironically, this little disaster happened right before my GP appointment to talk about my mental health. I was already stressed, already burnt out. Living far from you, in a cute but cold, overpriced flat. Friendless. Stuck in a job I hated.

Agathe said something – probably something trivial, like when you got mad at me for saying *yep* – and I lost it.

I spilled my guts to the GP: low self-esteem, constant sadness, guilt, social anxiety, difficulty making eye contact, and yes, the sunflower oil incident thirty minutes before. He recommended the double T's: tablets and therapy, like they did with you. I took his advice. And I haven't thrown anything since. No more outbursts.

Maybe I should stick to this non-violent streak and avoid plate-smashing for now. Who knows – maybe immersing myself in *The Walking Dead* will help me channel all the rage without causing any slippery floorboards. We'll see.

I'm definitely back in London – I just walked past a Mercedes-Benz parked next to a yellow skip with a Lime bike tossed in. Bizarre yet entirely expected. There's also that persistent cry of ring-necked parakeets – you'd love it. Sensory overload.

When I get back to the flat, I'll grab lunch with Agathe at one of the many restaurants in Ealing Broadway. Then it's game time: England's first match of the Euros against Serbia tonight. Must-win. No excuses. You'd be buzzing, glued to the pre-match punditry, scanning the team line-ups. I know you'll be watching with me.

In a bizzle, Samizzle.

FRIDAY 21 JUNE

Dad brought you home today, Sam. Your ashes are now resting in a casket pon di shelf – not the souvenir one, but the smaller shelf by the window, where your ventilator used to sit, under the charging point for Mista Hoistman. A cosy little corner for a not-so-cosy situation. The casket's wedged between your lamp and that big old pug teddy rocking your Iona Cruise Ship hat. Did you pop that hat on Puggy Dread, or did Mum or Dad do that after you left?

Dad sent me a photo of your ashes' new home after dinner while watching the second half of Poland vs Austria – like me, he's loving the Euros. Rarely misses a game. Football helps us feel closer to you.

He did it all on his own, Samwise: picking you up. I wanted to be there, and I feel bad for not managing it, but my full-time job makes it tough to come home every weekend. And Mum's been staying with her Trini cousins in Greenwich for a few days. She's being well looked after. She needs that.

Jamieboys couldn't wait any longer, though; he wanted to bring you back from the Chapel of Rest. It was tough for him to go to work in Winchester and then come home Han Solo, knowing you – in the form of ashes – were stuck in a dark room at the mortuary. It didn't sit right with him. So he picked you up earlier today. While he's glad to have you back at 12 Sidders, he's not pleased that you're now just a bag of dust instead of a hairy twenty-seven-year-old in a wheelchair. Sorry – that was a bit crass.

I'm on the Piccadilly line, heading towards Covent Garden. Agathe's bought two tickets for a ballet show at the Royal Opera House. Can you even call it a *ballet show*? I wouldn't know; I've never seen live ballet. I imagine I'll see plenty of pumps, tiptoes, tutus, and leggings, accompanied by an orchestra, while a well-dressed crowd claps politely and licks expensive ice cream during the interval. I don't know.

If you were here, you'd be a right old Envious Eric. You loved a good show, a fresh experience to add to your list of highlights. Can you hover next to me and The Frenchy while we watch the dancers prance around the ambient stage?

I miss you, brother.

I know, Brother Jack. I miss you too.

I'm on the tube avec Agadoodoos. The carriage is full. Seven souls sit opposite me. If you were here, I'd read them out to you like characters in a short story. I'll tell your soul instead.

- The Scribbler – jotting down notes like he's about to solve world hunger, but instead of a smartphone, he's using a notebook. Old school. I wonder what's troubling him.
- The Michelin Teen – A spotty teenager wrapped in an enormous puffer jacket with a furry hood. How he's not melting in this weather is beyond me.
- The Accountant – a woman with an exceptionally small nose and sharp eyes, flicking through a magazine like she's hunting for errors.
- Mick 'The Fisherman' Fleetwood – a yellow coat, scraggly white beard, bulging eyes. He looks like he belongs on a fishing boat, as well as behind a drum kit.

- Ballet Babe – next to Mick, dressed to impress in a floaty floral dress and bright pink stilettos. Probably on her way to the same show as us.
- Lady in White – head-to-toe in white, except for the black headphones clamped over her ears. Staring blankly out the window, contemplating life's big questions, listening to Billie Holiday or Dinah Washington – someone jazzy and soothing.
- Last but not least, Mr. Rosy Cheeks– in his sixties, clean-shaven with rosy cheeks, looking somewhat disoriented, like the tube's unfamiliar territory for him.

And there you have it, Sam: our seven seated strangers, each living out their own little drama, crammed together like a jury. I feel like the judge.

See you at the ballet, Sammy Elliot.

SATURDAY 22 JUNE

What do you want to know, Sam? What should I share with your soul, apart from strangers on a train? I'm at a loss for words. My brain's gone blank. I want to reminisce, to talk about you – but I just don't have the firepower.

Billy Bobs has eaten up all my energy. It's Saturday afternoon and I still haven't managed to switch off. I've been busy creating cardboard collagraph prints, inspired by traditional African masks, for my new printmaking project. Billy Bobs snubbed the collagraph technique as too simplistic, too infantile – well, I'm hell-bent on proving them wrong.

Well, I'm sharing something with you after all. The words found a way out. But now they're out, I'm back to feeling drained. Saturdays tend to do that. The weekend rolls in; my fuel runs out.

When I let myself think about you, it only adds to the fatigue. Being brotherless makes me sleepy. Maybe it's because remembering you brings me comfort – kind of like how Agathe lulls me to sleep, or how I do the same for her. We feel relaxed in each other's presence.

Or maybe it's the crushing reality that I'll never see or hear from you again. That really takes the wind out of my sails. Just typing that made my head feel heavy.

I'm slumping into the sofa now. Eyelids drooping. Sun shining directly on my face. That's all I've got for now.

Nap time.

REWIND

SUNDAY 23 JUNE

The last song you had blasting on Spotify was 'Rewind' by Paolo Nutini – I took a peek at all your open apps before returning your phone to the Apple Store. What a lovely little ditty, Sam; one I now find myself listening to on a weekly basis. And don't you think it's eerily fitting to our situation? I mean, I know it's technically a breakup song, but still. If only I could turn back time. And I know you'd want that too – to be alive again.

I want to do more rewinding in this memmy moir. I want to travel back to our childhood, to those days spent in primary and secondary school. You up for it?

Take me back, Jack.

Alrighty then.

Let's begin with Fair Oak, an itsy-bitsy village in the borough of Beastly Eastleigh. The first place we lived in together: a two-storey semi-detached house at the end of a quiet cul-de-sac called Stoke Heights – Stoke popping up again, see? I don't remember much about the house itself – the interior, the way the kitchen and bathroom looked, the colour of the walls – it's a blur.

Furniture-wise, all I can remember is that old green, floral-patterned sofa in the living room. and the bunk bed we shared in our bedroom with the colourful duvet covers. We were bunk bros! How much fun we must've had in that room, along with the inevitable arguments. Who slept where? I like to think I was on the top bunk, being the most able brother. You could still walk back then, unaware of wheelchairs or DMD, but climbing ladders would've been a challenge for you. You took your time getting up the carpeted stairs, dragging one foot up at a time.

You were my slo-mo bro.

Remember how we lived next to Stoke Park Woods? Dad would take us on nature-boy walks, and we'd wander along the chalky paths like little woodland creatures. He was all about the great outdoors.

I remember a younger version of Mum too, with dark black hair – still frizzy like it is now, but longer and curlier. Wild like the woods. She'd drive us to school, shopping centres, garden centres; we drove through many Hampshire roads with Mum behind the wheel of whatever car we had at the time. The cute lil Fiat Punto springs to mind. I can still see us in the back, pulling faces and miming along to pop hits on the radio, like 'Feel' by Robbie Williams, on our way to the big Sainsbury's for a shopping spree.

My most vivid memory hasn't got a lot to do with you, though, Sam. I was sitting on the front steps of our house after eating a large, gelatinous sweet, shaped like Heimlich the caterpillar from *A Bug's Life*. The chubby little caterpillar was revolting. It left me nauseous and gave me a headache. It was a bright, sunny day, and the combination of the heat and the sickly artificial fruit flavour triggered my first-ever panic attack.

I remember being short of breath and trying to breathe deeply but feeling like I couldn't get enough air. Dizziness set in, and I had to stumble inside for a water-chugging session. I felt like death for the rest of the day. Just thinking about that vomit-coloured caterpillar makes my stomach churn and my head spin. Ever since that traumatic incident, I've steered clear of re-watching *A Bug's Life*. And every time I see squidgy, gummy sweets now, they gimmie the heebie-jeebies – unless they're coated in sugar, like

Tangfastics. But too many of them can make my teeth all sensitive.

That's that, though – can't remember much else from our Fair Oak home. I know we had a little garden, but its appearance escapes me. We packed up in 2001, when I was around eight; you must've been about five or six. It was just a place I remember living in with you, Mum, and Dad, during the Upham Primary School days – the source of most of my early childhood memories.

That school was a visual feast, Sam. The green field where we pretended to be athletes on sports day. The little pond outside Mrs. Threlfall's office. Those Tupperware containers of watercress sprouting in Mrs. Brooks' classroom. The overhead projectors with hymns on acetate. The comforting smell of candles in the assembly hall. The vicar who'd pop by from the local church, bringing with him smiles and sunshine. The horseshoe couch where we'd watch *Fourways Farm* as a treat – what a show. The brick-red school jumpers, complete with the small white logo featuring a curved cross. The red-and-white gingham dresses that made the girls look like picnic tables. The burgundy book bags we lugged around like they were filled with secrets to the universe.

I can still feel that uniform – the softness of those jumpers and the heaviness of the grey trousers. We donned that uniform five days a week.

Upham bros.

I remember my deep brown hair, the front spiked up with too much gel, like Simon from *The Inbetweeners*, and your short, golden locks – not quite brown, not quite blonde. They were glistening, like you were an angel, not a Waddington.

I'd joke about you being adopted, but you never bought it. You knew exactly who you were. You were sure of yourself.

We'd shuffle out the front door, book bags clutched tightly in our small hands, ready for Mum to whisk us off to school – just a short ride from Fair Oak. At Upham, we went about our days separately, sticking to our own year groups. Your main pal was Dom.

Then there was Dom's older brother who was in my year. They were complete contrasts at primary school. His older brother, for whatever reason, wanted to see me dead, while Dom was the epitome of a supportive childhood friend – he even came to your funeral party with his mum. Such a nice guy. I think his brother's grown into a decent guy too, from what I've heard. Strange how life unfolds.

I still have nightmares about hiding in the toilet, though, tears streaming down my face, as Dom's brother and the scary kids in the year above rattled on the cubicle door, threatening to hurt me. That traumatised the shit out of me. And that was just the beginning of my experiences with big bad bullies.

What else springs to mind? Oh, my fake marriage! I fake married a girl with a West country accent, who was large and intimidating – much like her mother, who once called Mum saying, 'Your Jack's been hurting my Jess.' I likely got into a scrap with Jess, my wife-to-be; the details are hazy. She was tough, and I had developing anger issues – not the best mix.

It was a rocky marriage. If it had been real, it would've surely ended in divorce. I don't think I had much say in it, come to think of it. I remember her grabbing my hand one day in Mrs. Brooks' classroom, declaring that we were getting married at lunch. I wasn't great at saying no, Sam.

We used to laugh at what my then-wife's mum told our mum. One of the last voice recordings you sent me on WhatsApp had you whispering, 'Your Jack's been hurting my Jess,' in that charming Somerset accent. You were something else. You always knew how to crack me up.

You were well-loved in your year group, and I'm happy you had a strong circle of friends, free from bullies. Bullying is nasty business, and I was somehow a magnet to it; it left a lasting impact on me, contributing to the anxiety I still carry. I'm glad you didn't have to face that. You battled with the life-threatening condition; I battled with bullies. Just the hand we were dealt.

After Upham, I moved on to Kings' School in Winchester; you joined me there when I was in year nine. While I hopped on the yellow bus with all the other able-bodied kids, you rolled in solo in an accessible taxi. You weren't entirely on your own, though; you had a transport carer by your side. Sylvie was your sidekick during those rides – assisting you in getting in and out of the taxi, helping with your bags on and off your chair, offering conversations, and making that trip from 12 Sidders to Winchester a little less lonely. She was a sweetheart, always remembering your birthdays. You kept in touch with her until she passed away last year. Another person who cared deeply about you, Sammyboys.

I didn't see much of you at our humungous secondary school. Our time together at Kings' was short-lived – just over two years. The moment that sticks out the most there is when you were in year seven, and some punk told you to hurry up and move your wheelchair out of the way during break.

I wasn't next to you at the time – I was a bit further back – but I heard that spotty kid talk down to you, and I rushed over to confront him, telling him to leave you alone. Can't remember his reaction – probably muttered something and sulked off; he knew he was wrong. I told you to ignore impatient people like that. You said thanks, and then we went our separate ways to our next class.

I think that memory has cemented itself in my mind because it made me proud: sticking up for my younger brother – something I always wanted to do and still do. I've yelled at people on the phone, train staff, doctors, even random people on the street. Anyone who dared to treat you poorly or look at you the wrong way – only I get to do that!

I wish I could've stuck up for myself as fiercely as I did for you. Instead, I retreated and allowed myself to be an easy target. I had more friends at Kings' than I did at Upham, but the bullies multiplied too.

Life at Kings' was never plain sailing. Dodging footballs from the angry kids during lunch was a daily sport. Trying to avoid eye contact with the older kids on the bus, praying they wouldn't decide to use me as a punching bag – which happened more times than I'd like to admit. I felt like a lone goat in the Kings' grasslands.

One of the most traumatic moments was when this aggressive kid slapped me after a maths lesson, for no apparent reason. Maybe he just didn't like my face or shy, artsy vibe. I was walking down the stairs, heading to the school gates, because it was the end of the day, when I heard a flurry of footsteps behind me.

Turning around, I saw the boy accompanied by a couple of his whippersnapper friends. He pinned me against a wall and delivered a hard slap to my left cheek. They all laughed as they strolled away, leaving me stunned and with a burning face. I could still feel the imprint of his hand on my cheek during the bus ride home.

I wanted to keep this incident from Mum and Dad, feeling embarrassed and ashamed, not wanting to cause them worry, but I found it hard to conceal my emotions. When Mum asked me about my day, I broke down in tears. Mum, being Mum, immediately called the school to speak with my head of year. Go, Mum!

I don't remember the details of that call; I was likely hiding in my room with the TV blaring, too nervous to listen. The head of year, Mr. Parsons, spoke to me the following day and, with a smug grin, remarked on how Mum sounded Scottish on the phone. At the time, that really annoyed my fourteen-year-old self. I wanted to tell him to fuck off unless he was going to do something about me getting slapped, but looking back, it's rather amusing: Mum as an irate Scottish woman demanding justice for her son.

Unfortunately, we didn't get any justice. Mr. Parsons conducted an *investigation* into the incident, interviewing the boy and his friends who witnessed the slap – all of whom were confident and well-liked, particularly by the teachers. Typical arrogant poshos from well-off Winchester families.

The boy claimed he slapped me because I was being racist towards him, which caught me off guard when I found out. I had no idea how to be racist; the thought terrified me. The boy, who was from Pakistan, nonchalantly played the race card in his defence, and Mr. Parsons felt compelled to address this serious accusation.

Ultimately, my cowardly head of year decided that we were both at fault and issued a one-day exclusion for each of us.

I'm not sure if you remember Mum's reaction, but she lost her shit. Not with me, but with Mr. P. She called him again and released her Scottish temper, telling him how it was: that he'd made an incorrect decision, and that it was unjust for me to be punished for my innocence – which was true; I wasn't being racist in the slightest.

Let me tell you what happened in that maths lesson, Sam – I know you're already aware of the whole story, but I need to get it off my chest. And you're the best listener.

For whatever reason, nearly all of the boys in the class were singing 'Baa Baa Black Sheep,' just quietly enough to avoid detection by the teacher. Typical behaviour for childish teenage boys.

Feeling conscious I was one of the few boys not singing, and eager to fit in and gain some street cred, I decided to join in, making sure to keep my voice down. I stopped when the teacher looked towards me – I didn't like getting in trouble.

And that was it. That was my moment of being labelled 'racist.' Of course the boy didn't truly believe I was being racist: he simply saw a chance to hit a nervy kid who wouldn't retaliate. He picked his victim wisely.

That was Kings'. Your older bro getting dicked around left, right and centre, suffering in silence, crying himself to sleep, dreading going back to school the next day. Although I had friends and laughed and had positive memories, the bullying took its toll on me. When I think back to Kings', I think about pain.

Hanging around with you at home was my pain relief. We played FIFA, wound each other up, sang silly songs, and laughed at inappropriate things. We were brothers and best friends. Well, you were my best friend; I don't know if I was yours. It's ok if I wasn't. I won't be offended if you just saw me as your big bro.

You were my saviour, though, Sam. Seriously. Without you, I couldn't have made it through school.

Thank you.

MONDAY 24 JUNE

Today's message will be a short one, Samwells; I have a busy day ahead of me. First day of the school week. Four weeks until the summer holidays. I'm counting down the days now.

I'm about to walk up the big hill to work. Fifteen minutes until I reach the school gates.

So, back to our childhood.

After my time at Kings', I went to Peter Symonds, also in Winchester. We didn't see each other much during the daytime then – me working on my A-levels, you completing your GCSEs back at Kings'. Most of our brotherly moments were at home, before and after school/ college, or at weekends.

I can't remember who helped you shower on which days, but it was mainly me and Jamieboys – no evening carers back then.

I preferred college to school. There were fewer bullies, fewer subjects, and more freedom. I could finally let loose my sensitive, artsy self and pour all my energy into painting: huge, colourful canvas paintings inspired by David Hockney, Ken Kiff, the Fauvists, and my boy, Jean-Michel Basquiat – who I thought was an absolute king with his crown motif. I made paintings bursting with life.

Life was happening fast, and I was trying to capture it all: The Cure lyrics, blues music, medieval architecture, books, horror films, football logos, oil sticks, paint drips, black outlines, gradients, caricatures, The Waddington Brothers, girls I was smitten with, dreams, nightmares, naughty thoughts, countries, flags, instruments, patterns, animal skins, flowers, birds, monkeys of every kind···

I crammed it all in.

And when I wasn't painting, I was glued to FIFA. I was an addict in my late teens, no joke. I roped you into it too, didn't I? We played countless games together, either downstairs on the big TV – if Mum allowed – or upstairs on the tiny one in my bedroom.

Remember our joint career with Luzern FC? We turned that modest Swiss team into a European powerhouse, lifting the Champions League trophy multiple times. We co-managed: watching each other play, deciding on transfers, discussing tactics, or playing solo when the other wasn't around – always striving to perform our best, because we didn't want to disappoint each other.

We were inspired by Brian Clough and Peter Taylor of Derby County, who we learned about in the sports biopic *The Damned United.* Bottom of the second division to top of the first in just five seasons. Inspirational stuff for two young football-heads.

We also faced off against each other; you played as my opponent in my other career modes. Those matches were heated. I was determined to win since it was my career, and you were just as eager to beat me. Draws were rare. Losing frustrated us. There were times we played something daft like ten games in a row until we both had a win. A few controllers met my bedroom wall in frustration – the dents are still there. FIFA was our outlet for anger. We were frustrated and passionate teenagers, hammering buttons until peace returned.

You were physically stronger back then, Sam. We engaged in various physical activities, like play fighting and high-fiving. We also enjoyed table tennis duels at The Hub. On bright days, we'd trek there – you comfortably seated in your chair, me lugging your large bag with the folded KAFOS. It always felt like I was transporting severed robot legs.

But they were your transformer legs, your ticket to ping pong battles. We had a whole pit-stop routine before you could stand at the table:

- Step one. Kick off your shoes.
- Step two. Wrap cotton bandages round your thighs to prevent skin sores from the KAFOs.
- Step three. Strap on the KAFOs, lock the knee joints.
- Step four. Slip shoes back on.
- Step five. Carefully lift you upright, only releasing my grip once you were balanced.
- Step six. Penguin-waddle you to the table.
- Step seven. Grab bats and balls from the bag hung on the back of your chair.
- Step eight. Hand you a bat and ball so you could serve first – because I'm kind like that.
- Step nine. Dash to the opposite end of the table, bat at the ready, and shout, 'Right, let the games begin!'

We took it seriously. You never wanted me to go easy on you – you thrived on the struggle. It was your norm. Your life was one big challenge – nothing ever came easy. I'd send the balls flying to the edges of the table, forcing you to stretch and return them. You rarely let a shot slip by. Tough as nails, Sam. I had to graft for every point.

You know, if it weren't for Dooshy, you would've excelled in sports – perhaps as a tennis player or boxer. I'm certain of it. You had a knack for using your arms effectively and played by the rules. And you were also competitive. Like me. We often found ourselves in heated debates over decisions. VAR would've come in handy back then at The Hub.

We also swam at hydrotherapy pools around Winchester: The Pinder Centre, Naomi House. Swimming with you always left me in awe, as if I were witnessing a surreal painting come to life – an adolescent with DMD floating through the water. We played catch, and I'd pull you along while you held onto one of those long cylinder floats, letting you glide with grace, your head bobbing out of the water. Like a beaver. You enjoyed being buoyant in water. No muscles or weight to worry about. You were free.

The sea, though – that was another story. Tenerife, 2019. Our last family holiday, just the four of us, minus carers or Agathe. The beach was a man-made paradise: sparkling white sand and crystal-clear waters, complete with wooden walkways leading from the street to shore. And the bright yellow sledge that reminded me of a cartoon submarine, which the local lifeguards referred to as a *floating beach wheelchair*. It sounded and looked magical, and The Four Waddingtons were excited to try it out. And since there were no other bum-bounds around, it was our Sam's moment.

Without a portable hoist available, Dad and I had to carefully lift you from your chair using your ProMove sling. It was a delicate operation – one slip of the hand could turn a beach day into a trip to the local hospital. I took the left side of the sling, Dad took the right, and together we lowered you into the floating beach wheelchair. The friendly lifeguards strapped you in with care.

'Ready for the orcas, Sam?' I joked.

You chuckled, but I saw the nerves flicker in your eyes. Not because of the orcas – your most-feared animal. It was the sea itself that scared you. The idea of drowning. The open water wasn't your territory. Still, you were determined to take it on and bravely tick it off your bucket list.

The lifeguards wheeled you to the shoreline, handing you a long float, which you gripped tightly, knowing it was your lifeline. Dad and I stayed nearby, ensuring you felt secure from the start. Bodyguards in swim shorts.

Once we were sure you could paddle freely while holding onto the float, we let our guard down a little and watched you move through the water cautiously.

But as your swim dragged on, you began to feel overwhelmed. You paddled towards the safety of the shallow water and cried out, 'I'm going to drown! I'm going to drown!'

Dad and I exchanged a calm glance. 'You're not going to drown, Sam. You've got the float, us, the lifeguards.'

'Just watch out for Free Willy,' I added with a grin.

'No. Seriously,' you gasped, 'I want to get out now!'

And that was that. Your legs must've been knackered from all that treading. You were ready to call it a day. Dad and I guided you back to shore, signalling the lifeguards, who swooped in like Spanish superheroes, and soon you were strapped safe in the yellow boat again.

'That was fun,' you said, shoulders loosening.

'You've changed your tune.'

'Bit tired now, though.'

'Yeah, I bet. You had to really work those legs of yours, Sammyboys.'

'Yeah. Good exercise,' you chuckled.

I love the videos Mum took – you in full panic mode, thrashing about, screaming, 'Get off me, get off me!' Deep down, you must've loved it: splashing around in the warm water with your dad and big bro, Mum cheering from the shore, the four of us together. That was a proper day, Sam. One I'll never lose.

Billy Bobs looms into view as I reach the summit of this goddam hill. The blue gates stare at me like prison bars. Gotta be quick now.

So, after you left Kings': 2013. I buggered off to Camberwell College of Arts to study Painting, and you enrolled at Barton Peveril in Beastly Eastleigh. You chose Barton over Symonds as it was closer and better suited for students with physical disabilities. Fair beans.

You took a tasty trio of A-levels: English Language, Psychology, Media Studies, developed into a confident individual, and made lifelong friends in Harry and Ian, who became part of your inner circle.

You still loved a boogie, but singing and dancing on stage became less frequent. You were growing up, becoming a little more self-conscious. A Serious Sam emerged. Your performative nature shifted into public speaking. You enjoyed your role as a Student Ambassador and found pleasure in giving talks on Open Days. Bravo.

2015 – A-levels in the bag, then off to study Journalism at Winchester Uni, a field you had a fresh, new passion for. First time living away. There was no denying you found it difficult since you were a homebody through and through. But you stuck it out. You chased every opportunity you could: press officer at Winchester Ukulele Festival, *Daily Echo* internship, ambassador roles for Taking Charge and Pathfinders, where you spoke about living actively and independently with DMD.

You smashed it.

Boom. Your education years, wrapped.

I'm scribbling this from a cubicle in the staff toilets, eager to squeeze it all out before transforming into Mr. Waddington.

Speak later, Sambobs.

SATURDAY 6 JULY

Again, I'm lying in my bed at 12 Sidders, Sam. It's half-six, and a wren outside is making enough noise to wake even you. Funny how loud they are for such a small bird. Mum and Dad are still snoozing; they tend to get up later these days. I've been awake for an hour. My body's buzzing from my dream – or nightmare. I can't tell which. It had its ups and downs.

I saw you pull up in a black car with two mystery passengers. I couldn't identify them. It was a misty day, and when I spotted you, my heart sank – I thought you were gone, burnt to ashes. The car slid into a spot in a packed parking lot, looking like it belonged outside some American supermarket. I approached the car just as you stepped out on your own two feet. I've never dreamt of you walking before; it felt weird. You were my height too, like you'd been stretched. You smiled and wrapped your arms around me. You could lift them with ease – no sign of weakened muscles. We held each other for a while in silence, tears streaming down our faces. There was no trace of your life-threatening illness.

Then I woke up, gasping for air.

And now I need a hot shower to calm my nerves. But first, let me give you a quick update on why I'm here this weekend. I came back for the work shindig that SPECTRUM organised. It took place yesterday, from one to four. I took a day off work – I wasn't going to miss it, Sam. The Three Waddingtons were a little anxious driving over to your workplace without you – it felt like we were heading to your funeral party all over again.

We were pleasantly surprised upon our arrival. The cheerful receptionist welcomed us like we were royalty, had us sign in, and led us to a large function room. About thirty people were scattered around, nibbling on food from paper plates and pouring themselves cups of tea or coffee. I recognised a few familiar faces from the funeral party, but most were strangers. I felt a strong urge to thank all of them, but my shyness held me back, like it does with most of my ideas.

The grieving Waddingtons gravitated towards a blue table at the front, adorned with items you used to keep on your work desk: a large, fluffy pug toy, an open carton of lemon and ginger teabags, a cylindrical orange sharpener, and a small notebook filled with work–related notes in capital letters. I immediately flicked through the notebook. On the last two pages, you'd penned two limericks – one for me and one for Dad. You kept them quiet, didn't you, you cheeky leprechaun! A little surprise for us. I wish you'd left one for Mum too. Perhaps it's hidden in another notebook somewhere?

There was also a framed photo of you hustling at your stall during an event in Southampton Common, wearing your Love Don't Hate T–shirt. I couldn't help but feel a swell of pride. You found a job and made it your own. Above the table, photos lit up the big screen, and a playlist of your favourite songs hummed softly.

Although it felt odd, like a second funeral party, we held it together. We smiled and spoke with everyone who offered their condolences. Each person held you in high esteem, Sammyboys. Your absence is deeply felt at SPECTRUM. You made a significant impact on the local community, raising the alarm on hate crime and guiding people on how to tackle it and who to contact if they encountered it. Such an honourable role.

Council representatives and DJs from local radio stations were there too. I lost count of how many events and interviews you took part in. You zipped across the city, spreading awareness about hate crime and the support you could offer. You were a local hero. Everyone at your farewell raved about your dedication to your work, your ability to listen, and the enormous void your departure has created.

Absolutely nailed it, bro.

We spent a good few hours there before heading back. At 12 Sidders, Dad and I plopped down for two football matches in a row while Mum got lost in her art again – quite a familiar set-up now. I dozed off during a penalty shootout between France and Portugal, playing on your wall-mounted TV in your bedroom. We were sinking into a new green sofa The Parents splurged on. It's super comfy. It's taken the place of your profiling bed. Mum and Dad shuffled things around, making your room look all nice and cosy.

Don't worry, all your junk's still here: your souvenir shelf, your clothes, and those football scarves draped over the curtain pole. I sat in the corner beside your four framed movie posters – your all-time favs: *Harry Potter and The Philosopher's Stone*, *Interstellar*, *The Shining*, and the one and only, *Titanic*. Behind me hung our caricatures, drawn by the man with the ponytail at Leicester Square: me with my bulging Adam's apple and St Christopher necklace, you with your perfectly round head and little tash.

Your revamped room is a peaceful little nest I'm sure you'd approve of. I liked being there with Dad, watching the footy, surrounded by all your things. It felt like you were right there with us, nudging me to keep my eyes open for the penalties.

Mum still showers your room in kisses. Sometimes she sits on your new sofa and hugs your casket of ashes. I want her to continue to do whatever she needs to do to cope. It's all we can do.

FRIDAY 28 JUNE

Bom dia, Brother Sam.

I'm in a taxi headed into the heart of Lisbon. This weekend, I'm staying in a coastal town called Costa da Caparica, just south of the Tagus River. My old Upham Primary School friend, Tristan, is having a beach wedding. Really happy for him, Sam. He loves it out here with his little family. How cool is it that his kid gets to grow up in Portugal?

After you passed away, T-man and his fiancée, along with many other kind souls, donated generously to Naomi House. Altogether, we raised over two grand for the charity. Reading those heart-warming messages really got to me.

The wedding kicks off at four this afternoon. Agathe and I arrived in Portugal late last night and now we're shattered. But it's not stopping us from exploring Lisbon for a few hours before the ceremony. It's a little trip down memory lane. Being a Lisbonite for half a year was fun, but I doubt I could've handled it much longer. I kept complaining about the heat and the hills. And I was too far away from my main man.

As the taxi crawls through the crowded streets, I gaze out the window at all the familiar sights: restaurants and shops we used to go to, famous landmarks. That amazing pastel de nata shop. But I feel nothing. There's this hollowness gnawing at me. Your death has sucked the joy right out of my life.

Christ, that was dramatic. And maybe a slight exaggeration. I'm sure happiness will bounce back eventually. It just needs a little time. Hopefully it shows up before I head to Southeast Asia. I don't want to feel like a vegetable in Indonesia. I like travelling. I want to enjoy myself. I want to eat lots of nasi goreng and see wild orangutans in the Sumatran jungle. I want to lose my mind.

***

The wedding was a hit, Sam. Tristan and Camille put on an unbelievable show. After the church ceremony, I might have gone a bit overboard with the free cocktails and these lemon-flavoured shots of God-knows-what, so now I'm burrowed into the Airbnb bed with my head spinning. Agathe's fast asleep next to me; she drank a little too, but not as much as me. Sometimes I drink for the hell of it on special occasions, but it's rare.

The dinner was a feast fit for kings, with a killer view of the starry sea. Hugh, just like you would've done next year, delivered a whopping best-man speech that left everyone in awe. And I wrapped up the evening with a little beachside boogie with Agathe, who looked stunning in her bright red dress.

I feel so fortunate to have found such an amazing girl, Samwells. Sure, we squabble sometimes, but she da one for me. I'm thrilled to say that I'm marrying her next year, even if I'm a little terrified about the day. But the thought of having kids with her? That excites me big time. I cannae wait for our petit half-French Waddingtons. I joke that if we have a boy, I'll name him Bruce, which she hates. We need to agree on names that work in both French and English – easier said than done. A headache for another day, I guess.

But what really touched my heart that day, Sam, was during the church service. The priest paused to pay tribute to those who left us too soon, wishing them eternal happiness – and right at the very end, your name rang out, echoing through those tall, candlelit walls. In that moment, I felt you were there with me, smiling and laughing as you always did. Across a hilltop church in another country, surrounded by love and joy, you were remembered.

And it got me thinking about my own wedding. About how, when my turn comes, I'll find a way to have you there too. Maybe in a song, maybe in a speech, maybe in a framed photo on a table à la Aggy's dream. You'll be part of it, one way or another. Just like you were today.

You live on, my dear brother, Samwise Ganjapops.

Right, time for some tipsy dreams in Beddybyeland.

SUNDAY 14 JULY

Football final day, Sam. England vs Spain – yes, you heard it right: Southgate's somehow dragged the Three Lions to another Euros final! Let's hope we can clinch victory this time. I don't know how we got here, in all honesty. We've been playing so poorly this tournament. Spain, on the other hand, have been bossing it – winning all their matches with ease. Tiki-taka football. Bootiful to watch.

But our boys are better on paper: so many talented individuals. Cole Palmer, Jude Bellingham, Bukayo Saka – the list goes on and on. We had a decent semi-final, to be fair. Growing into the competition, finding form at just the right time. Crossing my fingers for tonight, Sammyboys.

Because you're such a Nosy Norris, I figured you'd want to know where I'll be watching the chaos unfold. I'm at a pub in Chiswick called The City Barge. It overlooks the Thames and Oliver's Island. Sun's out, and seabirds are flapping their wings outside. Delightful stuff.

When I walked into the snug pub, I asked if they had any seats for the game later, ideally near a TV. The friendly barman guided me to a table right in front of a wall-mounted TV – just like the one in your bedroom. He could sense my satisfaction.

'Enjoy the match.'

'Thank you. I will with this seat. Best in 12 Sidders – pub, I mean.'

The bartender chuckled. 'Will you be having lunch here?'

'Oh, yes please. Can I get a fish and chips?'

'Of course. And something to drink?'

'An Earl Grey tea, if you have it.'

'One fish and chips and an Earl Grey tea. Will that be all?

'Perfect, thank you.'

The bartender smiled and headed to the bar to relay my order.

Fifteen minutes later, the food arrived promptly with three colourful sauces: curry, mushy peas, and tartare – all top-notch.

I'm diving into *Paula* by Isabel Allende as I digest my food and sip my tea. What a book. Finally picked it up from my bookshelf. The Chilean writes so well, Sam. I'm determined to read every book by her before my time's up, like you did with Roald Dahl. I may be on my own here at The City Barge, but I'm in my happy place.

Hugh and his girlfriend will swing by later, just in time for the kick-off. Agathe might make an appearance too, but she's footballed out and is enjoying some peace at home. I'm an eager beaver. I set up shop four hours early – worried I wouldn't find a seat. You'd either be impressed or think I'm nuts. Hard to say.

I enjoy my own company. I'm used to it. Gives me a chance to unwind and reflect. Saying that, I wouldn't say no to your company right now. That would make this whole experience even better. We could feast on a massive pub meal and geek out over tactics. If only.

***

Getting hyped now. I'm walking along the Thames Path, stretching my legs, and jamming to your party playlist: *Sam's Party Playlist.* Currently vibing to 'Get It On' by T. Rex. Banger of a tune. So cheeky. Reminds me of *Billy Elliot.*

I've been sitting stubbornly at my table in front of the wall-mounted TV for over an hour. Still three hours until the match starts, but only an hour and a half until the programme begins. Can't miss the pre-match build-up. I'll head back to the pub soon. Just soaking in the views and savouring the fresh air.

Canada geese are waddling by on the riverbank. I can spot a little egret in the distance and a couple of cormorants gliding eastward. You'd be impressed by my ornithological knowledge. You'd be lounging in your chair, catching the sun rays, wearing those orange-tinted sunglasses, caked in sunscreen, while I point out all the birds. You'd nod and say, *That's great. Well done, Jack. You know a lot about birds.*

Kylie Minogue's 'Love at First Sight' is playing now. You wanted a party, Sam! Are you throwing one in heaven? What's it like up there? Pearly gates and clouds galore? Cheesy tunes and seafood buffets? Does heaven even exist? Are you a god? *The* God?

There are a fair few Spaniards around; they're making me tense. I want to tell them they're going to lose the final – this is Englerland's year! Feeling super patriotic, I am, Sam.

Righty-ho, old chap, I'm walking back to The City Barge now. Texting while walking, not looking where I'm going – I almost collided with a little girl in a yellow hat. Her parents shot me a disapproving look. *Watch where you're going, skinhead.* Fair point: I'm not being careful. I'm frantically writing to you. This is when I really need you.

You had a knack for watching where you were going. You couldn't afford not to. Bumping into someone in your wheelchair was a no-no – especially a child.

Ok, Sam, speak soon. Go on, Engerland!

AIRBORNE

FRIDAY 2 AUGUST

Sorry I haven't written to you in over two weeks, Sam. My bad. But guess what? We did it. Dad and I climbed the Ben. Ben Nevisissimo, as we liked to call it – we had this weird fondness for slapping *-issimo* on everything, didn't we? Our favourite suffix.

We're truly crushed now. You better appreciate the blood, sweat, and tears we poured into that climb. It was the ultimate father-son road trip. Hampshire to The Highlands – one country to another. Nine hours each way. We slept in a quaint market town called Kendal in the Lake District on the way up. On the way back, we swung by our beloved Stoke-on-Trent. We left The Potteries this afternoon. Dad's just dropped me off at Oxford before heading to Beastly Eastleigh. I'm catching a train to London since I didn't want Dad to drive into the capital just to drop me off; that would've been a nightmare detour.

I'm on the train now, suitcase in tow and Emma Bridgewater bag by my side – we stopped off at the famous factory on the way back. Agathe's building a collection of crockery and wanted me to pick up a few discounted treasures from the outlet. I ended up buying her three mini mugs, which are carefully wrapped at the bottom of the bag.

I also have a packet of ibuprofen and paracetamol in my pocket. I'm dealing with a bad earache. I think it's infected. There's discharge and swelling and it's making me sick thinking about it. Great timing, hey? Two days of holiday with a throbbing left ear. I think it's a combination of trapped water from my shower and the pressure change while we ascended the Bennyboy. Anyway. It didn't ruin the holiday, but you know how I'm a wuss when it comes to pain. I can't wait to get my hands on some antibiotics.

I'm not the only one feeling rough. Dad was practically sleep-driving as we approached Oxford. I felt bad for not being able to share the load with him, but I still don't have my driving licence. One day I'll get it··· maybe. Probably not, actually. I'm not particularly enthusiastic about driving. And there are too many cars on the roads already. Nevertheless, having that skill would've made this trip smoother for Dad.

The driving and the mountain trek took its toll on him. His whole body aches, especially his calves. Before we left, he'd been dealing with hip issues, and despite the concerns expressed by family members – Mum and Granny in particular – we weren't worried because we knew he'd get to the top. He was our superhero.

We organised this trip to Scotland so he could take on the challenge. His dream of climbing Mount Everest with his dodgy hip wasn't realistic. This was the best alternative. He felt it would be a waste to travel all that way across the border without trying. So he bucked up the courage and gave it his all.

On the day of the climb, he was among the few brave over-sixties attempting to conquer Britain's highest peak. I felt proud to be his son when we reached the summit. Although hesitant at first, he utilised the walking sticks he'd bought for support and didn't fall once. I was right there with him every step of the way, especially on the descent – advising him which rock to step onto, steering him from the edge, terrified he might slip into the abyss.

We had to take our time since he couldn't skip down the steps like I could. His movements were careful and measured, which made the climb take far longer than we'd expected. We started our ascent at nine-thirty in the morning and returned to the car at half-seven in the evening. Nine hours of climbing on a sunny day with hardly any shade. Incredible. We also ran out of food – we didn't anticipate being outdoors for that long.

Dad performed a miracle that day, Sam. I'm sure you were there with us, guiding him up and down that daunting mountain. You must've given him some of your spinach.

Now he's feeling the aftermath. He plans to take it easy this weekend. He has 12 Sidders to himself – Mum's on holiday with Swardy at the seaside in Essex. They're enjoying themselves, and our mama needs that. Too much time at 12 Sidders can be overwhelming for her.

I hope you're not haunting the house, Sam?

***

The other day, just before our trip to Ben Nevisissimo, something wild happened. Mum only went and smashed a plate right outside the house! I couldn't help but watch, laughing and egging her on. She took a poor old dinner plate and tossed it onto the paving slabs outside 12 Sidders. Crazy mama. She said she wanted to smash something to let out her frustrations, and I totally got it. Grief was aggravating us.

With a playful spirit, she went outside and let the plate crash onto the concrete, causing a beautiful explosion of porcelain shards – as if she was channelling Julian Schnabel. Job done. Afterward, I cleaned up with a dustpan and brush, feeling somewhat responsible as it could've been me if I wasn't trying to work on my anger management. Remember the oil?

I need to rest my eyes now. I'm feeling a bit shivery from lack of sleep. Last night, I only managed about two hours of snoozing due to my earache.

Speak soon, my special little bro.

TUESDAY 6 AUGUST

Hi Sam.

It's a cloudy day in August, and I'm lounging on the sofa, lost in a spin-off series of *The Walking Dead* called *Fear the Walking Dead.* I've devoured all eleven seasons of the original.

I'm crying a little, feeling sorry for myself. It's not just the ear infection – the blocked ear escalated into an infection, which I'd suspected might happen. I've got antibiotics to treat it, but they've wiped me out, and my sleep's still a mess. I'm too tired to cry during the day, so I save my tears for my dreams. Most dreams feature me bawling my eyes out. I guess I need to release it somehow.

I cry because I feel completely lost without you here. My best buddy – the one who gave my life meaning – has vanished. You've been deleted without the option to undo.

I hope you're able to walk now, like the undead on my laptop screen. Not stumbling around clumsily in search of flesh. Confidently striding, stretching those bad boy legs of yours. Maybe that's what you're up to – walking freely. Perhaps you'll go for a run, or a swim, if there's a pool or beach around. Get that heart pumping. Work up a sweat.

As for me, I feel completely unmotivated. It's been far too long since I last exercised, and my belly bulge is getting bigger. A few weeks ago, I joined a local gym, went once, saw guys flexing in the mirror, felt awkward as hell, and never returned. I have a tendency to start projects and then abandon them before truly committing.

My ADHD medication arrives next month, just in time for the new school year at Billy Bobs. Not gonna lie, I'm kind of looking forward to going back; it's been a decent distraction during this time of grief. It's important to have something to focus on. I'll also be mentoring a trainee teacher, so I need to have my head straight. And I'll have a bigger room with a sink and more storage space. And no mouldy ceiling. Exciting times on the horizon.

Strange how these neurodivergent minds work – how perspectives shift. Just a few months ago, I couldn't wait to see the back of Billy Bobs. I was all about that posh girls' school in Kingston.

Remember when I learned to drive a few years ago? I lost interest quickly due to the costs and gave up. Am I a quitter? In some respects, yes.

I'm not keen on working at this London school – or even teaching art in secondary schools – for much longer, but I can't find the drive to search for something new. I want to buy a property, but I'm unsure where to live. London's enchanting: offers a slice of everything, but I'm torn about staying. At the same time, I can't picture myself living anywhere else.

I tend to see flaws in everything, Sam, including myself.

I want to get married, but I'm shit-scared of standing up and speaking in front of people. I'm a nervy bastard with social anxiety and I don't know how to live with it. I fear commitment, making decisions, and completing projects – like this book. Sometimes, I just want to run away from it all and give the world a middle finger.

But I won't.

I've decided – literally right now – to finish this book tonight. It won't be easy; my ear's pounding, and my eyes feel heavy, but I need to wrap this up. I've been hiding behind these words for too long, focusing on them every day since you left, seeking solace and safety in them, forgetting what the world outside looks like.

The words have served their purpose, for the time being. Now it's time to muster up the courage to engage with my life. I need to peel myself away from my laptop and phone and find new sources of comfort.

You'd agree, Samwells. You'd say I'm fixating on you, obsessing over you. Writing has been a useful outlet, but it can't be my only refuge. It can't last forever. It'll wear me out. My little brother was a lot – writing about him every day is a lot. I mean this in the best possible way.

I won't fib and say how happy I am now, one hundred and fifty days after you checked out. I refuse to sugar-coat my struggles. This shit's ongoing. But I do see some progress. The tears come less often – when I'm awake, that is. I catch myself smiling more. Laughing too, especially with The Parents. It feels like it's getting easier – or at least it seems that way. I need to trust myself. Time to put down my final full stop and cross that finish line.

At first, I thought I should wait for something significant to happen before I said goodbye to this book. Until I'd *seen* you.

But what the hell was I expecting? You're not coming back. No one's cloning you. And I'm not ending my life to join you in whatever comes next because I feel guilty being able to breathe.

Life will trudge on – you gone, me mourning. I'll carry this grief; it's part of me now. I can't even remember what I was like before this happened. I'm living a second life, I swear. Kind of cool, in a way. It's like I've been reborn.

So maybe choosing to sign off on a random, overcast Tuesday in August is the wisest way to go about this.

With you no longer here in the flesh, it's just Agathe I feel myself around now. The weird, guard-dropping self. Not a lot of people, is it? I'd like to be around others – opening up and hanging out for hours – but it's just too exhausting. It requires too much brain power, so I shy away from it and retreat into myself. Then loneliness creeps in.

Happiness is a rare visitor these days, and when it does knock on the door, it often brings Sadness along with it. And he never takes his shoes off. The mucky bugger.

And this heavy bag of grief isn't going anywhere. I've accepted that. I never truly believed it would disappear like you did. It's something I must learn to carry. Losing you is a scar that will never fully heal. But that's ok. I've made peace with it. I'm determined to embrace this reality. I'm not going to give up.

The grief will feel lighter as I grow older and stronger. I know it will. I have to keep going. I need to build a future for me and Agathe. There's so much more waiting for me. Like children. Maybe they'll have some of your traits, like your love of lists and collared shirts.

You would've wanted to continue living and embrace more adventures. You were a traveller and a survivor, just like those in *The Walking Dead.* And so am I. I must keep moving forward. I need to find reasons to smile. Memories of us giggling will inspire me when I need a bruv-nudge.

I'll eat more of your spinach too. You stocked up on that veg like you were expecting an apocalypse. You would've thrived in a zombie outbreak, Sam – no doubt about it.

I never found it easy being on this planet. I've always felt like a clumsy intruder, knocking into things, getting it wrong, apologising for taking up space. Yet, I manage. I live. I fight. I endure.

You're with me every day, stitched into my thoughts alongside others I care about – Agathe, Mum and Dad, and even myself. I won't take a shortcut to reunite with you. I refuse to surrender. I'll keep going. I'll keep building. Living life to the fullest until my time comes, just as you did.

I'll continue my earthly journey and see you when I see you, Sam.

THE END

Dedication:

For Sam

Acknowledgements:

To the team at ShadowScript Publications and Book Hub Publishing – thank you for taking a chance on this project and trusting me with Sam's story. Niall, Susan and Conor, I'm incredibly grateful for your belief, guidance and patience throughout this process.

To my friends and those who read the early drafts of this book – thank you for giving your time, honesty and encouragement when the pages were still finding their shape. Your steady support throughout this journey has meant more than you know.

To the Duchenne community – your strength, generosity and support have meant everything. To Muscular Dystrophy UK, Action Duchenne, Duchenne Family Support Group, Naomi House and Jacksplace, and Sibs Uk – thank you for sharing my work and for continuing to support families like ours.

To my mum and dad – thank you for giving us a childhood full of memories, laughter and love. And to our wider family and friends, thank you for standing beside us in times of need.

Agathe – my angel through all of this. You have carried me through the highest highs and the lowest lows. Without you, this book would not exist in the way it does. I am the luckiest man to call you my wife.

And then you, Sam. My forever brother. My best friend. The kindest person I have ever known. Thank you for everything.